African Writers Series
Editorial Adviser · Chinua Achebe

95
The Smell of it

The Smell of it
& other stories

by Sonallah Ibrahim
translated from the Arabic
by Denys Johnson-Davies

HEINEMANN

Heinemann Educational Books
48 Charles Street, London W1X 8AH
P.M.B. 5205 Ibadan · P.O. BOX 45314 Nairobi
P.O. BOX 3966 Lusaka
EDINBURGH MELBOURNE TORONTO AUCKLAND
HONG KONG SINGAPORE NEW DELHI
KUALA LUMPUR KINGSTON

0 435 90095 1 (*paper*)
0 435 99400 x (*Arab Authors*)

© Sonallah Ibrahim and
Denys Johnson-Davies 1971
First published in African Writers Series 1971
Reprinted 1978

First published in Arab Authors series 1978

Printed Offset Litho and bound in Great Britain by
Cox & Wyman Ltd, London, Fakenham and Reading

Contents

1 The Smell of it — 1
2 The Snake — 59
3 Arsène Lupin — 77
4 Across Three Beds in the Afternoon — 87
5 Songs of Evening — 109

The Smell of it

تلك الرّائحة

This race and this country and this life produced me ... and I shall express myself as I am.

James Joyce: *Portrait of the Artist as a Young Man*

The Smell of it

'What's your address?' said the officer.
'I haven't got one,' I said.
'Where, then, are you off to? Where are you going to stay?' He looked at me in amazement.
'I don't know,' I said. 'I have no one.'
'I can't let you go off just like that,' said the officer.
'I used to live on my own,' I said.
'We have to know your whereabouts,' he said, 'so we can come and see you each evening. A policeman will be going with you.'
And so we went out, the policeman and I, into the street. I glanced round curiously. This was the moment I had continually dreamed of throughout those past years. I searched within myself for some unusual sensation, of pleasure or joy or excitement, but found none. People were walking and talking and moving quite naturally, as though I had always been with them and nothing had happened.
'Let's take a taxi,' said the policeman.
I told myself that he wanted to have an outing at my expense. We went to my brother's place. On the stairs we met my brother, who told me he was just going

The Smell of it

away, and that he had to lock up the flat. We walked down and went off to a friend's.

'My sister's staying here,' said my friend, 'and I can't take you in.'

We went back into the street. The policeman began to grumble; a savage look came into his eyes. I thought to myself that he was wanting ten piastres.

'We can't go on like this,' he said. 'Let's get along back to the station.'

At the station there was another policeman. He said: 'You're a real problem and we can't just let you be.'

I sat down in front of him, putting my suitcase on the floor, and lit a cigarette. Night came and he said he was unable to do anything. He called over a third policeman and said to him, 'Lock him up', and they led me off to a locked room with a fourth policeman standing at the door. He searched me and took my money and pocketed it. They then put me into a large room which had a wooden bench raised slightly above the floor along the walls. I seated myself on the bench. There were many men there and all the time the door was being opened to let in yet more. I felt a pricking on my neck. I put my hand up to my neck and felt a wetness. I looked at my hand and found there was a large blob of blood on my finger. The next moment I saw dozens of bugs on my clothes. I stood up. For the first time I noticed the large splodges of blood that stained the whole of the walls.

One of the people there laughed and said to me: 'Come here.'

Some of the people were sitting down on the floor. One of them had spread out a torn blanket on the floor.

The Smell of it

I found myself a small corner on the very edge where I sat down, resting my chin on my knees.

'Why don't you go to sleep?' the owner of the blanket said to me, but there wasn't room for my whole body to lie down on it.

'I prefer to sit like this,' I said.

Someone else asked me: 'Drugs?'

'No,' I said.

'Larceny?' he said.

'No,' I said.

'Murder?'

'No.'

'Bribery?'

'No.'

'Forgery?'

'No.'

At a loss, the man lapsed into silence and proceeded to give me odd looks. I began shivering with the cold, then I stood up and walked about a little. I sat down again. Tired from the way I had been sitting, I shifted my position. One of the men produced a blanket which he had kept folded up under him and began preparing for sleep. I began amusing myself by hunting for the bugs that were running along the floor and killing them. Suddenly I lowered my head over my chest. I didn't want them to see my face. They had begun to give themselves up to sleep. In front of me an old man had stretched out to sleep on the bench. The policeman opened the door and called out to him: 'There's someone asking for you.'

The old man came back carrying a blanket and a pillow and stretched himself out on the bench, covering

The Smell of it

himself up with the blanket and leaning his head against the pillow; soon he was asleep, breathing loudly and paying no attention to the bugs.

Alongside him there sat a man who was staring into my face, his hands plunged into the pockets of his overcoat, which was undone, his chest naked, for he was wearing nothing under the coat. Suddenly this man let out a strange frightening howling sound; he got up and approached me swaying; he laughed into my face, then sat down alongside me, staring in front of him distractedly; then he gave another howl, and a young, heavily built man got up and struck him in the face.

'Don't hit me,' said the madman, lifting his arm to protect his face. Blows from the young man rained down on him. I heard his bones crack. He fell down where he was, breathing heavily. The others laughed.

The owner of the blanket pulled it over himself and spread it out with his hand over a plump young boy who was sleeping beside him. I saw the boy's face before it was covered over by the blanket. He had a bronze complexion and full lips. He was immersed in sleep, his knees flexed. The man encircled him with his arm under the blanket. He began moving until he was right up against him. I watched his arm under the blanket as it moved over the boy's body, stripping him of his trousers. The man's thighs pressed against the boy's back. Alongside the boy sat the heavily built young man who had struck the madman. He was following what was taking place underneath the blanket, raising his eyes continually to meet mine. After a while the movement under the blanket quietened down. The cover shook and the boy sat up, wiping his

The Smell of it

eyes as he roused himself from sleep. He began looking down between his thighs. I dozed off as I sat there, then came to again. I didn't see the heavily built young man, then I caught sight of his thighs from under the blanket. He was asleep, hugging the boy to him. I got up and walked about, and the blanket shook. The young man dragged it from off the boy and wrapped it all round himself. The boy slept on, his thighs naked.

The darkness began to lighten. I watched the light of dawn spread. At last they opened up so we could wash. They took the boy away to make him clean out the courtyard. The rest brought out food and breakfasted.

The boy appeared at the door and asked: 'Haven't you left me anything?'

'No,' said the heavily built young man.

The policeman began calling out names. I heard my name. I took up my suitcase and went out. I found my sister waiting with the policeman of yesterday. He handed me a small book bearing my name and a photo of myself. We went out, my sister and I, to the street.

'Do you want anything to drink?' said my sister.

'I want to walk,' I said.

She took me to a flat in Heliopolis. Collecting some clean clothes, I went off to the bathroom. I locked the door behind me and took off my clothes. I stood naked underneath the shower. I rubbed my body over with the soap and opened up the shower above me. Raising my face, my eyes stared up into the small eyes of the shower. The water gushed down, forcing me to close my eyes. I lowered my head and followed the soap flowing down my body with the water, then running

The Smell of it

on to the floor along to the drain. Closing my eyes, I stood under the water, motionless. I turned off the tap. I took up the towel and slowly dried my body with it, then I put on my clothes and left the bathroom. I lit a cigarette.

'Let's go to the cinema,' said my sister, and off we went. It was a film about birds that grew in number and size until they became savage, chasing people and attacking children. I was conscious of having a bad headache. We returned to the flat. My sister started energetically cleaning it, while I moved between the hallway, the kitchen, and the bedroom, smoking, and avoided going near the window. I took off my clothes and stretched out on the bed, then the bell rang, and I got up to answer it. It was the policeman.

'Just a minute,' I said to him and hurried off to the bedroom and came back with the book, which I gave to him, and he wrote his name against the date and left. I returned to my bed and lay down. I lit a cigarette. I began staring up at the ceiling. I remained stretched out on the bed without sleeping. I smoked a lot.

Morning came and I got up, washed, dressed, and went out. I had a sandwich and bought all the morning papers, then I took a Metro-train. I watched the carriage doors as they closed. I stood alongside the apartment reserved for women and began scrutinizing them one by one. They had elaborate hair-do's and their faces were heavily made up. I got down at the First Aid stop. A man was lying on the pavement beside the wall covered over with blood-spattered newspapers, while on the tram-stop platform in the middle of the street a number of women in their black milayas had gathered, gesturing towards the man and wailing. I got on to the bus to Muna's house. Her mother met me. I kissed her hand. To begin with she didn't know who I was. We sat down and talked. I had to talk to her about her husband. I told her I'd been with him until the last moment.

I was sitting beside him, my hand manacled to his. We were at the back of the lorry and the other lorries were behind us. He knew what was going to happen, but he didn't say anything. He kept humming to himself a stanza from an old love song. The wind was bitingly cold and there was nothing to protect us from it. I began to shiver and my teeth chattered. We couldn't see where we were going at all. We began to talk about Hemingway. In the darkness I saw him take a comb from his pocket and comb his hair which was full of grey. I knew that he used to dye it to hide the grey hairs. Silence reigned in the lorry. In front of us Ahmed wrapped a towel around his head, moaning. As he shivered frenziedly, his headache tore at him. When we arrived it was dawn. They drove us out of the lorry with sticks. We sat on the ground. We were shuddering with the cold and fear. He was the tallest one of us. I heard someone say: 'That's him,' and they struck him on the head and said: 'Lower your head, you dog.' They began calling out our names. Then they called his, and that was the last time I saw him.

'Can you imagine,' she said, 'I got a letter from him before that. He said it wouldn't last long.'

I told her that he always used to tell me that he never went to sleep at night without imagining he was hugging Muna in his arms. He used to clap his hands and say 'I'll get out before you'. He wanted to be free at any price.

Muna's mother glanced around her wearily and her

swollen lids closed over her eyes. Her head sank down into her short flaccid body. She motioned to me to draw nearer.

'Did he really love me?' she whispered.

'Of course,' I said to her.

What should I say to her? What was the point of going into the matter all that precisely when everything had come to an end? Also who knows exactly what goes on inside another human being? They say that some people are created for love, others not. Other people say that love is only to be found in novels. He himself recounted to me once the story of a woman whose relatives had chased him off with cudgels because he was of a different religion. Then there was another woman, but she had died suddenly. There was a third one who, he had discovered, had come to an agreement with her husband on the necessity for having a child by any means. He was past forty-five and getting on for fifty and wanted a child. One day we were sitting in the sun together and he was lost in faraway thoughts. I was chatting away, while he was preoccupied. He was not listening to me. Perhaps he was working things out in his mind. Once, though, I was going down the stairs beside him. We were approaching the ground floor and we heard the sound of a quick staccato tapping on the stairs. Then in front of us there appeared a tall girl who came to a stop in front of the lift door. The sunlight was falling on her face from the window-panes on the stairway. She looked towards us. She was laughing for some reason and her hair was ruffled. Her cheeks were red and she moved about restlessly. He was going down the stairs beside me, his eyes on her. I heard him give an ardent sigh.

She went off to her room and came back carrying a small wallet from which she extracted some papers.

The Smell of it

She handed me a ragged sheet of paper, saying: 'This is a poem he wrote for me before we got married.'
(*Always she looked as though lost in thought, and when he asked her what she was thinking about she'd say: About life and death.*)
He wrote:
>*I'm sad, my little girl,*
>*Sad and alone.*
>*In a bed I sleep,*
>*A bed cold and dead.*
>*With no one to talk to,*
>*With all the books read,*
>*With no one to laugh with,*
>*Without tears to shed.*
>*This is death,*
>*Only worse,*
>*For when we die we're unable to think*
>*Unless worms think.*
>*And when you're alone you think,*
>*You yearn, you seek and strive,*
>*And know not what you're striving for.*
>*This is life and death.*
>*It is not life at all*
>*Except that I have not yet died.*
>
>
>*But hush! Here are footsteps coming,*
>*Human steps.*
>*They are coming, they are drawing nearer*
>*Are they real? Yes! No! Maybe!*
>*Yes! Here they are, ringing the bell,*
>*I hear human steps.*

The Smell of it

> *I hear human voices*
> *Radiant with laughter.*
> *A friend? No, more than one.*
> *They are friends, my little girl.*

> *I am no longer sad, my little girl,*
> *But yet am frightened,*
> *For they will go and leave me once again*
> *To life and death!*

The bell rang and Sakhr came in. He had shaved off his moustache, his hair was combed, and he was carrying all the morning papers under his arm. The bell rang again and a smart young man entered.

'This is my husband's friend,' she said to him and pointed at Sakhr.

'I know him,' said the young man.

At once Sakhr got up, put on his glasses and began walking round the room. There were some English and French books on a shelf and he began looking through them; putting a hand to his waist, he took one of the books over to the window where he opened it and began going through the pages as he looked at the young man from time to time from over his glasses.

It must certainly have been one of the happiest of moments for him when he had felt that there was someone who had got to know him for a particular reason. In the past he had believed that everyone knew him, then he had discovered the truth gradually. When I saw him for the first time he was bare-

The Smell of it

chested, walking along slowly and every now and again raising a finger to stroke his moustache. In those days the world's leaders grew moustaches in a variety of shapes. It was no coincidence that every one of them had a different-looking moustache. Then it was discovered that these moustaches were cheats. With their owners gone, the fashions went too. Nothing remained on in the heart. Not once had it been filled. He began striking his head against the iron door until he almost split it open. And he was weeping.

From the window I saw a girl in the house opposite embracing another girl and kissing her on the lips. A girl who was blind in one eye entered the room and began crying. Sakhr began stroking her hair as she wept. The lady said the girl was like that, no sooner did she see a man than she would weep.

At last Muna came back from school. 'I'm Daddy's friend,' I said to her, and she looked at me with hostility. I took her to the club. There were other children there. I asked them to take her into the water with them as I didn't know how to swim. They took her with them and she began romping about and playing happily. There was a piece of wood to help people swim. She got hold of it, but another fat little girl grabbed it from her so as to swim off on top of it. Muna clung to the piece of wood. The fat little girl took her by the hair and pulled it fiercely to make her let go of the piece of wood. The fat girl took the piece of wood and lay on top of it. Muna was now a long way from the edge of the pool and I quickly ran along in her direction. She was bobbing up and down in the water, puffing violently, her eyes wide open in terror. I called to her, but she sank below the water and didn't

The Smell of it

appear again. One of the swimmers rushed to her rescue, dragged her out, and brought her to me.

I took her home. As we were going up the stairs she said to me: 'When there's anyone around I'll say that you're my father, so don't say you're not.'

When we entered, her mother was dressing, so I waited for her. My eye lighted on the wall-clock and I jumped to my feet, rushed to the door, and hurled myself down the stairs to the street: the policeman was due at any moment. I arrived at the door panting. I found a letter awaiting me. I looked for the sender's name and saw it was Nagwa. I went upstairs again and read through the letter slowly. I lit a cigarette, stretched out on the bed, and read the letter again. She was wondering whether we couldn't meet up again after all these years. I closed my eyes and pictured her, what I was able to recapture of her: tender eyes and a full mouth.

The bell rang and I got up to answer the door. It was the policeman. I asked him to wait till I went back to my room; then I brought him the book and gave it to him to sign, and he left. I kept the book in my pocket for the next time he should come. Again the bell rang and when I opened the door I found Nagwa standing in front of me. I embraced her. She hugged me to her violently and pressed her whole body close up to mine. But I did not press my body against hers. I pushed her away from me and looked closely at her. I led her off to the bedroom and put out the light, sat on the bed and seated her beside me. I drew her towards me and kissed her on the lips.

She turned her face away and said, 'Talk to me.'

The Smell of it

I had no desire to talk. I passed my hand over her face, which was hot and soft. She turned to me and said: 'Speak. Tell me what happened.'

I put my hand on her mouth, drew her head towards me, and kissed her. I took hold of her lips between mine and she too bit me in the same savage, unsophisticated manner. She moved away from me.

This is what always happened. The first time I kissed her she was shy. I was sitting beside her and the light was falling on her cheek; we stopped talking, and I rested my head against her shoulder but she didn't object. I kissed her on the cheek. Then on her lips. When we had plucked up courage a little she took hold of my lower lip and bit it savagley. I felt pain. I wanted to feel the softness of her lip in my mouth. I could never have enough of her: had I been able to stay on embracing her for the whole day I would have done so. There was a warmth in her face and thighs. After each time I would make her stand naked so that I could gaze at her thighs. They flowed beautifully and softly in their brownness, and I would ask her to bare her arms to me so that I could kiss them and feel them against my body. But she used to have qualms. In the dark we would lie and press up violently against each other so as to forget the world and everything in it. We'd no longer think about anything or feel frightened of anything. When my cheek rested against hers and our noses were touching, our heads close together and our eyes on one level staring up at the same place on the ceiling, nothing had any importance any more. The next moment my head would move and my lips would come surreptitiously towards hers and we would exchange kisses, sometimes gently, sometimes violently, then she would move her head away and sigh. The first time I hugged her roughly to me she said: 'Where were you all this time?' The

The Smell of it

second time she said: 'Darling,' and I remained silent as the word rang in my ear for the first time in my life, while I didn't believe what was happening to me. All too soon she would turn round and say: 'I want to go to sleep,' and I would remain lying on my back with my eyes fixed on the ceiling, hoping she would suddenly turn round and embrace me. Soon I would feel her regular breathing, the breathing of someone asleep, contented and satisfied. I would turn my head and sit up a little in order to look at her. Her head would be lowered, resting on her arm, fast asleep; her hair spread out around her head, her other arm stretched over the side of her body. I would pass my gaze along her whole body, then lie back.

She stretched herself out beside me. She rested her cheek in her hand. She gave me her face which was lit up by a slice of moonlight.

'I'll talk to you,' she said.

She talked a lot, then she was silent.

I pulled her towards me, but she moved away. I asked her to bare her arms and she did so. I kissed her arm and shoulder in the moonlight.

Presently she said: 'It's cold.'

I covered her up. She lay stretched out on her back. She was certainly thinking about the same thing as I was. But something was lost and broken up.

'I want to go to sleep,' she said.

I pulled her towards me and kissed her. My lips wandered across her cheek, right up to her ear. I kissed her ear and went on until she shivered and raised her eyes to me.

'This too – where did you learn this?' she said.

How was it she had continued to remember when I had forgotten? When my lips had travelled up her thigh and I had

The Smell of it

kissed her there for the first time and she had looked at me with a mixture of joy and astonishment and embarrassment, and said: 'Where did you learn this?'

I stretched out my hand to her breast, but she pushed it away and said 'No'. I let her be and lay down beside her. I waited for her to turn round to me suddenly and hug me to her, but she didn't. I remained awake. I had a feeling of pain between my thighs. I got up and went to the bathroom. Having freed myself of my desire, I returned and stretched out beside her. I slept and awoke. I slept again.

When I opened my eyes the next morning I found her dressed.

'I'm going out now,' she said.

'When shall I see you?' I said.

'I'll pass by,' she said.

I continued to lie stretched out on the bed. Eventually I got up and had a wash. I got together my dirty clothes and put them in a tub of water to which I had already added some soap powder stirred up into a thick lather. My sister and her fiancé came along. I got into my clothes and we went out. I bought the morning papers. In the entrance to the house we met my sister's friend and her uncle. We went to the Casino Café.

'We'd like to see you married,' said my sister's fiancé.

'These things take time,' I said.

'Why?' he said.

'Love isn't that easy,' I said to him.

'Take my advice,' he said with a shrug of the shoulders, 'love comes after marriage.'

The Smell of it

'I've been married five times,' said the uncle.

I left them and went off to see Sami at his home. They took me into the living-room. I waited for a long time. A small child entered the room who I realized must be his daughter. She stood beside me. I was tired and wanted to go to the lavatory. I broke wind and the child smelt it. 'There's a smell of kaka,' she said.

I affected to pass it over, but she repeated: 'Smell of kaka.'

I began sniffing round myself and saying 'Where?' to her until the smell had disappeared.

In the end I gave up hope of Sami coming and I got up and left. There were large crowds of people about. In the street the radio was on full blast and I heard an English song about children and discovered that it was the same new song Mohammed Fawzi sings.

I got on to the Metro. The crush was terrible and I was almost stifled. I watched the tired faces of the women with their kohl running. I went to Samiyya's house and found them eating. Samiyya smiled when she saw me and said she had waited for me a long time before eating. I almost asked her: 'Really?' Instead I asked about her child, and she said he was sleeping. I felt myself smiling. Her smile was simple and frank. I had not imagined her to be so simple and gentle.

And then what? She has her husband and her child and no room for anyone else in her life, and all too soon I shall go away and that will be the end of everything.

Every now and again she would give a deep sigh.

'Oh God,' she said.

'If Freud could hear you,' I said to her, 'he'd have had something to say to you.'

16

The Smell of it

'All sorts of things,' she said.

We finished eating and she got up. She was wearing a flimsy blouse with nothing on underneath. From under her armpit I saw a part of her breast at the point where it rose up from her chest. I was surprised to find that it did not droop. It was white as milk. I quickly turned aside my gaze. I looked into her frank, unequivocal eyes. She went off to have a sleep. I too slept.

When I got up I looked around for her and went to her room. The bed was at the far end of the room. She was lying on her back, with the back of her head pointed towards me, her eyes facing the wall opposite to me, while her child sat by her breast staring around him in sleepy bewilderment. Her thigh – as white as milk – was bare and she covered it quickly. She got up and put on an orange-coloured dress and we sat on the balcony. She told me that her child loved me. I adored her soft, confident voice and her gestures which were so unaffected.

'Are you afraid of growing old?' she said to me.

I wanted to speak; all the time I was wanting to burst out into words.

'I feel I'm an old man,' I said. 'Seldom do I smile or laugh. Everyone I see in the street or in the Metro is glum, unsmiling. What have we to be joyful about?'

We talked about books. She said she had given up reading some time ago, ever since having the child.

'Have you read the novel *The Plague*?' I asked her.

I felt that much depended upon the answer she gave. But she said: 'No.'

The Smell of it

I thought of telling her I envied her her simplicity and gentleness.

I looked at the clock. I had to go. I stood up and she too stood up.

'Do you know,' I said to her in a low voice, 'that you're really strange.'

She looked at me in astonishment.

'I discovered you today,' I said to her.

She bent over her child and was engrossed in adjusting his clothes and I did not see her eyes well.

Her husband came. I said good-bye to them both. They followed me to the stairway. At the garden gate I looked behind me. Samiyya was entering the quiet, cool house and I watched her orange-coloured dress as it disappeared behind the door. I walked home. I saw a pretty girl walking slowly, as though finding difficulty with her shoes, alongside the rails of the Metro. I went into the house. I found the wooden room in the entrance lit up, its door open. I took a stealthy look inside and found Husniyya, my sister's friend, there. I went up to my room. My sister came along.

'Samiyya's nice,' I said to her. 'Is she happy with her husband?' I asked her.

'Yes,' she said.

'I bet she doesn't love him,' I said.

'Impossible,' she said. 'Where else would you find a man like him, both as a person and from the point of view of position?' Then she said: 'They used to meet up together before marrying.'

And so what if they used to meet up together before marrying? She was twenty-seven years old. She had waited in vain for the knight of her dreams for a long time. At home she used not to

The Smell of it

have a room of her own. She used to sleep in a room which was more like a hallway. She was never able to lock the door of her room and be by herself, to take off all her clothes, for example. She never kissed her body before the mirror. It was no longer possible for her to bear the way her father and mother looked at her every night. There was never any subject of conversation apart from the awaited husband. She was blamed for not having been able to get herself one. Then one evening she met him at the house of one of her girl-friends. The next day her girl-friend told her he wanted to marry her. After ten minutes' walk to the gate of her home, and at the door of the flat with its cracked paintwork, she said to her friend: 'And why not?' Maybe the beloved she had been waiting for was all an illusion. Maybe all this talk about love and the meeting of eyes and tremor of souls was nothing but so many phrases out of novels. Perhaps she would find happiness with him. Perhaps – the word that hangs over every new marriage – perhaps this was the awaited man. Perhaps love would come. After one year came the child and thus her everlasting bondage was completed. She had no choice but to resign herself. Then there was that time when the wireless was on and I noticed a faraway look in her eyes and her face wore a stamp of sadness. What had happened after marriage? I imagined them side by side in bed: one of them bored and irritated. One of them would remain throughout life feeling that some part of him had not been stirred, that some part of his flesh and blood had not been touched, that a well in the depths of him had not been tapped.

'Do you know what love is?' I said.

She looked at me in astonishment: my question was naïve and fatuous.

'Of course,' she said.

'Do you love your fiancé?' I said.

The Smell of it

'Yes,' she said. 'When we first got engaged I couldn't bear him, but I've come to love him with time,' she said, raising her voice.

'Why are you shouting?' I said to her.

'That's my normal voice,' she said.

She said she wanted to have a bath but that if she did her hair would be spoilt and she would have to go again to the hairdresser.

The bell rang. Carrying the book, I went to answer the door, but it was my sister's fiancé. Behind him came her girl-friend Husniyya.

'Imagine it,' said Husniyya to my sister, 'my fiancé's jealous of my uncle.' She said: 'He says I spend all my time with my uncle.'

My sister's fiancé said that he had been looking at a heater. He had bought the fridge.

'Does anyone know someone who's going abroad who could bring me back a tape-recorder?' he said.

Husniyya's uncle came along and took them all off to the cinema.

I remained on my own in front of the desk. I tried to write. The bell rang and I hurried to the door, hoping that something, anything, might happen; that someone, anyone, might come. I found the man from the ironing establishment.

Once again the bell rang. When I opened the door I found myself suddenly facing Nihad and her father. They at once came into my room.

'You must come to our place tomorrow,' they said.

'You've changed a lot,' I said to Nihad.

'The last time you saw me,' she said, smiling tenderly, 'I was very young.'

The Smell of it

They refused to sit down, saying that her mother was waiting in the car.

I saw them out, then returned to my room. I began smoking voraciously, while I thought and was incapable of writing, She had been scrutinizing me closely. I imagined she had heard a lot about me and was fascinated by what she had heard. For the third time the bell rang. The ringing was long and strong. Taking up the book, I went to the door and opened it. I gave the book to the policeman, returned to my room, turned off the light, and stretched out on the bed. I fell fast asleep, then awoke suddenly to the sound of the bell. When I opened the door I found no one there. I returned to my room, leaving its door ajar. Again I went to sleep.

I got up early the next morning, shaved, dressed, took a clean shirt off to the ironing place, returned and put it on, then went down and began looking round for a place in which to have my shoes shined. I bought the newspapers. Finally I took the Metro. The driver stopped *en route* to put a piece of hashish into his mouth and have a drink of tea. I thought him lucky, for he had found something to have recourse to in facing up to life. He continued to drive slowly, while I wished he would hurry up so that I wouldn't be late and the dust spoil the smart way in which I was dressed.

I got off a long way from the house and took a taxi. The taxi put me down in front of the house. I looked up at its balconies but saw no one there. I went up to the top floor and found Nihad with her mother seated before a table. They had not seen the taxi. I sat down beside them. Nihad was studying. I regarded her

The Smell of it

closely. Her lips were as I liked them: the lower one curved and the teeth slightly protuberant. Her voice was gentle and quiet. Her mother asked me what I was doing now. She talked in a loud voice. I told her I was writing.

'Are you writing stories?' she said.

'Yes,' I said.

'Out of books?' she said.

'No, from my head,' I said to her.

'Then you're really somebody,' said Nihad.

I lit a cigarette.

'You must settle down,' her mother said.

'America's wonderful,' said Nihad. 'What do you think?'

'Some things I admire,' I said, 'others not.'

'Leave all this,' she said, 'look after yourself.'

Then she said: 'Help me with my studying.' Her voice was low. I was tired of loud voices.

'Imagine what they did to my father,' she said. 'They threw him out of his company after they'd taken it over.' She said that they had ganged up on him and accused him of acting fraudulently.

'Let's eat,' they said, and we went down to the lower floor. We sat down at table and I put some salad followed by some rice on my plate.

'Leg or breast?' Nihad asked me.

My sister had warned me saying, 'Be careful not to take the leg because you'll never know how to eat it with knife and fork.'

I don't know how it was that I impetuously said to her: 'Give me the leg.'

She put it before me and I took up the knife and fork

The Smell of it

and when I sought to plunge the fork into it it leapt up in the air from my plate and landed in the salad bowl.

'Chicken shouldn't be eaten like that,' said Nihad. 'Eat it in your fingers.'

I told her my sister had warned me but I hadn't heeded her warning. Her father began to eat his leg of chicken with knife and fork. The mother said to me that in Europe people didn't eat the leg with knife and fork. After that I didn't know how to eat it. I dealt clumsily with the macaroni and the water-melon.

'Are you happy with the present state of affairs?' they said.

The father said he had met some people who had come from Russia and that the poverty there was terrible. He said that capitalism was better.

'Can there be any argument about that?' said Nihad fervently. Then she said: 'Do you believe in God?'

I got up and washed my hands and dried them on a towel. We went up to the top floor. They offered me cigarettes but I had no desire to smoke. The father had a conversation on the telephone. He was wanting to buy up the adjoining piece of land. The mother put her hand on her cheek and went into a daze. The father came in to have a sleep.

'Are you tired?' said Nihad.

'No,' I said, and we went back to going through her lessons.

The father rose from his sleep and came along and spread out his prayer-mat in front of us and performed his prayers, then he seated himself down beside us and tea was brought.

The Smell of it

'How's Nihad getting on?' he said.

'Fine,' I said.

The mother began copying out some of the lectures for her in her notebook. Behind us they turned on the television with the volume well up. The maid came, and the cook and the governess, and they all sat on the floor and watched. Nihad was paying me no attention and was following the film.

'Ahmed Ramzi's marvellous,' she said.

I began to feel tired. She got up and seated herself beside me. Her bare arm was alongside me. She was careful to see we didn't touch each other. Her mother heard me explaining an English word to her.

'No, that's not the meaning,' she said.

The father intervened, knowing only French, and said that the French word had another meaning. I didn't speak. The mother and father had an argument and the mother sought my support.

'Usually that is the meaning,' I said.

'No,' said the father, giving me a look.

'Roughly,' I said.

The din had become violent. Nihad said that a producer had seen her that morning and had said that she resembled the film star Lubna Abdul Aziz. Some visitors entered. Nihad got up to welcome them and sat herself beside them at the far end of the room. She would talk to them with warm intenseness, and then turn away from them to follow Ahmed Ramzi. I felt a headache splitting my head in two. I got up to leave. One of the women visitors looked at me enquiringly.

'I'm so-and-so's son,' I said.

She laughed and pointed at her nose and twirled an

The Smell of it

imaginary moustache upward. 'Was that the man with the great big moustache?' she said.

'Yes,' I said.

'I want you,' called out the mother.

Would she lean over and give me five pounds? I thought to myself. She signed to me to follow her to her room. Her maid was sitting on a chair. She was a plump, dark-complexioned girl. 'This one is my class,' I said to myself, and I thought that were I to talk to the mother I would be able to marry this girl. They would say they'd done me a service by finding me a wife of my own sort.

The mother passed me a roll of paper, saying that it was a length of cloth. I didn't know what to say. I had decided to refuse if she tried to give me money. I hadn't reckoned on cloth. I was embarrassed and refused, but she insisted and said: 'You're like a son to me,' and I didn't know how to behave, so I took it, saying to myself, 'Well, at least I got a suit out of it.'

I returned to the drawing-room. Nihad accompanied me to the stairs. I went out of the house and didn't look up. I walked and my shoes filled with dust and I didn't care. I took the Metro. The crush was terrible and my clothes got creased. I didn't resist. At one of the stations dozens of workmen returning home hurled themselves on to the tram and pushed their way through the crush. One of them stood himself in front of me. His eyes were bloodshot. Another propped himself against the arm of a seat and gazed blankly out of the window. He began to fall asleep. When, a moment later, I looked at him his head was jerking up and down to the movement of the tram and each time, sunk in

The Smell of it

sleep, it would bump against the support. When I got off the tram I caught sight of the same girl I had seen before, walking slowly alongside the tramline.

I went up to my room. I put the key in the lock. The same door and key among the same families of our class. I entered and undressed, putting my trousers on the clothes hanger and hanging them up on the wall. I had a bath. Then I returned and sat down in front of the desk. I turned on the transistor radio. I saw the roll of cloth in front of me and opened it up. I found it to be a length for a pair of pyjamas not a suit. I lit a cigarette. My sister came along and asked how much of the fifty piastres was left. I calculated the fares, but didn't have the courage to mention the ten piastres for the taxi. Her fiancé came and said he'd stood for two hours in front of the Co-operative to buy meat.

'The situation is quite unbearable,' he said.

'They're wanting to spread poverty,' he said. 'I've got no chance of making any money. If I were to build anything up, the government would only take it.'

Adil and his wife came along. I offered him a cigarette and he said: 'I don't smoke or drink coffee.'

Only in the morning, he said, did he take a cup of tea at home, and even so his bill at the office was as much as thirty piastres a day with all the cups he stood other people.

He said that unlike the other employees he never took bribes.

'More's the pity,' said his wife.

'No one knows how to talk to the workers any longer,' she said.

The Smell of it

Adil said that the chauffeur of his uncle Fahmi Bey didn't get up before ten in the morning, while Fahmi Bey himself was up at dawn.

'I'll show you the best place to buy a soap-dish.'

My sister said that she needed a servant, but where could she get one from? Her fiancé said he'd asked someone coming from Beirut to bring him a Ronson lighter.

'We must go now,' they said.

They left and I remained on, sitting in front of the desk smoking. Then I got up and put out the light. I stood by the window breathing in the air. My window overlooked the backs of several houses. Only a small segment of the road was in view. I craned out and twisted my neck round so as to be able to see the illuminated shops and the people coming and going. Tired, I drew in my head and rested my arm against the window-sill. There was a dark window opposite that suddenly lit up. Within it a girl appeared and began slowly to undress. At last she stood there completely naked, then threw herself on to a bed in the corner of the room. She lay on her face, her back to the light. I saw the curve of her body and the dark shadows left by the light in its folds.

Suddenly the bell rang. I took up the book and dawdled about a bit, lit a cigarette, and took the packet along with me. Again the bell rang. I hurried to the door and opened it to the policeman to whom I gave the book, while I extracted the packet of cigarettes and gave him one. He left.

I returned to the room and threw the book on to the desk. I looked out of the window and found that the

The Smell of it

other window had grown dark. I lay down on the bed, smoking till I had finished the cigarette, when I threw it out of the window and went to sleep.

In the morning I went out and bought a newspaper, a small bottle of milk, and some bread. I returned, boiled the milk, put some sugar in it, then dipped the bread in the milk. I read the paper. Then I went out again. I took the Metro. It came to a stop before the First Aid station and all the passengers got off. I found that there was a carriage turned over on its side near to the rails and that its black entrails protruded. I walked to the café in which Magdi used to sit. He was sitting in a corner by himself.

'We must affirm our existence,' he said.

I gazed at the wrinkles that had dug their lines into every part of his face.

'They are all of them sons of dogs,' he said; 'with people together you're strong,' he said, 'but by yourself you're weak,' and the muscles of his face contracted.

If you looked at him you wouldn't know if he was experiencing bitterness or pain. Is there anyone who does not know bitterness or pain? From the desire to dominate and from weakness in facing up to the world. From being bereft of love and from an inability to deal with it. From contempt for people and from the need for them. From the sensation of being subjugated and from practising persecution. From the suffering of pain and from the enjoyment of inflicting pain on others. From complete confidence and from the sensation of failure. From extolling the need to love people and from exploiting them like so many bricks with which to build your house. From the conviction that everyone loves you and believes in you and from seeing them

The Smell of it

abandoning you. In the beginning it was a matter of high-mindedness and it has now become a curse. The spring which used to suffer for others has dried up. When he stood with the blood dripping down his back, he was defiant, unshaken, finding a pleasure in his ability to hold out. But people no longer attached any importance to this today, for the spirit of the age had changed. It was no coincidence that the words he used had lost their meaning a long time ago, some having become almost totally meaningless. He was taking part in the game, understanding its rules and abiding by them. But they applied the rules against him and tears flowed over a lonely seat where he sat. The most dreadful thing is to start searching for yourself too late. He said that he had never loved. He believed that he was better than the others – and perhaps he was, there's nothing to stop that being so and he had given his all – but he was defeated at a game that knows no mercy, doesn't in fact have any rules, and in which you cannot decide what is correct and what wrong and in which the victor is not necessarily the person who is in the right but he who is cleverer, more cunning and possessed of more luck.

I left him and went off to the magazine. I walked down along the corridor, looking into each room but finding no one. There was a room in front of me at the end of the corridor. As I approached I saw a woman sitting at a desk, her cheek resting on her hand. I glimpsed tears in her eyes. I turned round and went back the way I had come.

I walked in the direction of the Metro and boarded it. I sat beside the window. When we left Ramses Square a train came alongside us, travelling in the same direction. It was full of soldiers returning from the Yemen. They were cheering and shouting and waving

The Smell of it

their arms at the windows. When the Metro was opposite them they got more worked up as they looked in on the passengers. The latter regarded them with stolid indifference. Little by little the soldiers' enthusiasm died down. The Metro had now overtaken the train. I turned my head round. The soldiers' hands were dangling out of the windows of the train. I saw one of them throw his cap to the ground.

I got off in front of the house and saw the beautiful girl who every day walked alongside the tram lines and discovered she was lame. I bought some food and went upstairs. I found the door of the flat open and my neighbour repairing the lock in the door which had gone wrong. I went in, ate, then smoked and went to sleep.

When I got up I found my sister had come. I went into the bathroom, took off my clothes and turned on the shower. I heard the sound of the door knob falling on the tiled floor. I turned off the shower, dried myself, put on my clothes, then left the bathroom. There was a continuous sound of tapping against something. I stood talking to my sister as I combed my hair. Again I heard the tapping. I noticed that it was a tapping on the wall.

'We always used to do this,' I said to her, 'when we wanted to send messages or warnings to each other.'

That used to happen every morning. We'd open our eyes to the measured sound of tapping on the wall. We'd jump to our feet. We'd plan everything and try to remember not to forget anything, though sleep still lingered in our eyes. We'd squat down by the wall, shivering with cold. The tapping would stop. We'd wait. Then we'd hear their feet on the stone floor. The rattle of

The Smell of it

chains and keys. We'd leap back to our places as the key struck against the lock. Then they'd come in. Our eyes would fasten on dull, expressionless eyes. Our ears would be struck by abrupt, rapid sounds that didn't let up. Our hearts hung upon hands that were heavy, stout, cruel, and unthinking, and around us the walls met at four corners. The door was locked, the ceiling near. No way of escape.

I went out into the hall. I happened to look at my neighbour's room. Its glass door was closed. I noticed his shadow from behind the door and his hand hammering violently against the glass. I found the key of the door lying on the ground. I picked up the key, put it into the door, and opened it for him. In a state of tears he told me he had forgotten the key on entering and that for an hour he'd been hammering for me.

'You must visit Husniyya and you'll see her fiancé,' said my sister.

We went off. Her mother welcomed me and said: 'You must settle down.'

'Marry him off,' she said to my sister, 'and he'll quieten down.'

Husniyya's fiancé came along. He said he'd arranged his desk at the Ministry marvellously. He'd got a large sheet of thick glass covering it. On the right was a fine desk diary he'd got from abroad, while in the centre was an ivory ink-stand the likes of which were no longer to be had. On the left was a place for the urgent files, while above his head was hung a calligraphic representation of the name of the Almighty. I told him that the sun was about to set and that I'd have to be off. I left them and hurried home.

I met the policeman on the stairs.

The Smell of it

'You're late,' he said.

I took out the packet of cigarettes but he shook his head.

'You could spend tonight in jail,' he said.

I took out ten piastres. He accompanied me to the flat; I entered, brought him the book and he signed it and left.

I slowly undressed, washed my face and made a cup of coffee. Then I tidied up the desk and wiped away the dust that had gathered on it. I seized hold of the pen but was unable to write. I took up one of the magazines. There was an article about literature and the sort of things that one should write about. The writer said that Maupassant said the artist must create a world that is simpler, more beautiful than ours. He said that literature should be optimistic, throbbing with the most beautiful of sensations.

I got to my feet and went to the window and looked out at yesterday's window. However, it was closed. Again I sat myself at the desk. I seized hold of the pen but was unable to write. I closed my eyes. I imagined yesterday's girl with her white body lying before me on the bed, full and rounded, her hair fresh and fragrant, while I kissed every part of her, passing my cheek along her thigh and resting it against her breast. I put my hand down to my own thigh and began playing with myself. At last I gave a deep sigh. Tired, I sprawled back in my chair, staring vacantly at the paper in front of me. After a while I got up and gingerly stepped over the traces left by me on the floor under the table. I went to the bathroom. I washed my socks and shirt and hung them up at the window. I turned out

The Smell of it

the light after leaving the door open so as to be able to hear the policeman when he came. I lit a cigarette and stretched out on the bed. I went to sleep. In the morning I went to my brother's house. Wrinkles had advanced across his whole face and his skin was full of white blotches.

'Everything's gone to pieces,' he said, 'since the workers became members of Management Committees.'

They said we should go up to the top floor to see his elder daughter.

My brother had built the villa fifteen years ago. He said it was his wife who had bought the land and it was the first time he'd known she had any money. At that time my father was still alive. He used to go along every day to supervise the building. We had lived in a cramped room. My brother completed the building, letting off the first floor and living in the second. Then he married off his eldest daughter and let the third floor to her. When his youngest daughter got married he moved out of the first floor and rented it out to her. He remained in the middle with his wife. In the beginning he would spend an hour every day in the garden, watering it, cutting the grass, and smoking his pipe.

She asked me whether I would read to her husband. Her husband said that Sheikh Abdul Basit had told him that praying in the Al-Aqsa Mosque was reckoned to be worth a thousand meritorious deeds. They said that we should go down to the bottom floor to see the younger daughter. She met us at the door, carrying her child on her arm. His eyes were close together.

'Isn't my son lovely?' she said.

She laughed, going on and on so as to excite her

The Smell of it

husband. He was standing beside her as he fondled the stars on his uniform. He said that if an ordinary soldier opened his mouth he'd slap him across the face to shut him up.

'It's high time you got yourself married,' he said.

'Be like me,' he said. 'The important thing about a girl is her background.'

They turned on the television.

My brother stood up straight in his aba and smiled and said:

'Have a look at this film.'

The film told the story of a girl who left a young boy of her own age and fell in love with a middle-aged man. When the film ended my brother looked at me superciliously. He took me to his room. He locked the door, then took out several old files. He sat himself at the desk and lit his pipe. He showed me some stories he'd written and others he'd translated, also some articles under the title *To you, milady*, a book about bodybuilding, another about the battles of the Second World War, and a third about Prince Omar Tousoun; also an old picture of himself in a hat and smoking a pipe in the garden of some house, and another picture with a German girl which he said was taken in the days when Rommel was drawing near to Alexandria and he had begun to learn German. He showed me a third picture taken in the office of an American company, and a fourth in an Egyptian import office.

'I'd like to get myself a really young girl,' he said.

He said he'd never been in love. He said that yesterday he had wanted to sleep with his wife but she had refused because he had made her buy the fruit out of

The Smell of it

her own money. When he gave her two pounds she had opened her arms to him. He gathered up the papers and pictures and returned them to their files.

'I've finished now,' he said. 'I shall breed rabbits.'

They summoned us to eat. I left and went off to the magazine and met Sirry. He told me he wanted to help me but that circumstances didn't make it possible.

'Have you read my articles?' he said. 'I'm the only person who writes like this nowadays. Fouad is a nondescript man. Imagine, he said about me that I'm his pupil!'

I left him and went off to Sami's room at the end of the corridor. This time I found him.

'I haven't any idea what you have written,' he said to me.

I stood by his desk while he was writing. Suddenly he raised his head to me and said: 'We won't hold you up. Come in and see me in a couple of days' time.'

I went out into the street. I walked to the Metro. I saw an extraordinarily beautiful girl through the window of an airline company. I got on to the Metro to go home and didn't find a spare seat. I stood looking at the people around me. In the carriage reserved for women I glimpsed part of a woman's face. She was looking down from the window. She was wearing a white sleeveless dress and looked very clean. She had doubtless taken a bath before coming out. Her hair was long and soft and had not been straightened at any hairdresser's. Beside her I spotted a little girl. My heart missed a beat when she turned her whole face in my direction. I saw her dark-brown complexion. Her face was without kohl or make-up. Suddenly I found

The Smell of it

myself looking right into her eyes.. They were wide and limpid. For an instant I was lost.

Her eyes were two stars in silent space. I was swimming in space, lost. It was night-time when our eyes met. Her two eyes gleamed in the light. I saw my image in their vast whiteness and I saw it in their deep blackness. Her arm was bare beside me. Her complexion was dark, infused with rouge, and she appeared flushed. I yearned to stretch out my finger and touch the full roundness of her arm just below the shoulder. Her blouse was white and flimsy. She was not wearing a brassière for I could see the nipples of her breasts on the blouse where they rested against the silk. Her complexion was soft. Her lips were full, the lower one slightly separated from the upper and in a cupid's bow; it was dark-coloured as though inflamed by something. When she was looking at me and smiling our eyes would meet and I would become confused. When I embraced her the first time she was silent for a while, then pushed me away from her. We were sitting in the dark. She stretched out her hand to my head and began fondling my hair. Then her hand slipped down to the neck of my shirt, then to my back and she began to explore it with the palm of her hand. And when I hugged her to me and buried my head in her neck, I enjoyed for an instant the softness of her skin against my cheek. I began breathing in her smell of cleanness – then I raised my head slightly and kissed her on the mouth. I felt giddy. When I wanted to do it again she pushed me away from her. I learnt to discover in her other things: when she would purse her lips and fall back into silence whatever happened and I would almost go mad trying to find out why; when, sometimes, she would appear kind and tender and I would worship her; and when I sat in front of her, my eyes fixed on her face, her hands, her legs, I would almost weep with desire for her. I knew pain

The Smell of it

when I used to look at her bright eyes and luscious cheeks, and when my fingers stole along her arms and my thighs would draw towards hers, she would refuse me. The last time I had almost gone mad. I had begun to be certain that she didn't care for me. She took me between her arms, allowed me to touch her breasts and hands, to kiss her cheeks and lips. But she was cold.

But she soon turned her eyes away. After that she didn't pay me any more attention.

I got off in front of the house and bought some food. I entered the house. I found there was a light on in the wooden room in which Husniyya's uncle sat. The door was open. When I looked through it I found him resting his head in the palms of his hands and contemplating the picture of a girl in a gilt frame on a small table in front of him. The picture was of Husinyya. In the picture her eyes were large and ravishing. I moved away before he should become aware of me. I went up to my room and undressed. I turned on the transistor radio but found no singing or music and it began to crackle. I sat down and tried to write. Black spots had made their appearance on the floor as a result of my moment of pleasure. Hassan came along and I told him that we should without fail get hold of a woman for tonight.

'I'll try,' he said and went out.

He returned half an hour later.

'My brother's on the stairs,' he said, 'and he's got a girl with him.'

'Keep yourself out of sight for a while,' he said, "cos we told her there were only two of us.'

'Have no fear,' he said, 'she can't refuse you so long as she's paid her price.'

37

The Smell of it

I went off to the kitchen and prepared the tea. Hassan came along. He said that his brother and the girl were at present in my room. I carried the tea to the hallway and put it on the table. We sat down near the table. Hassan lit a cigarette and began tapping on the table. After a while the door of the bedroom opened and his brother came out. I shook him by the hand. I hadn't seen him before. He was a large man in his forties. Hassan went into the bedroom. I offered his brother some tea.

'How are you?' he said to me.

'Fine,' I said.

Pointing to the bedroom, I said to him: 'What's she like?'

'Not bad,' he said with a shrug of the shoulders. He said: 'We toured all the streets in the car but we couldn't find anyone else because it's so late.'

Hassan came out and said to me: 'Your go.'

I took him on one side and said to him: 'I won't be able to.'

He looked at me in astonishment: 'How's that?'

'I don't know,' I said. 'I've got no wish to.'

He shook me and said: 'But you must go in. This is a serious matter.'

I told him I realized that but that I couldn't.

'Come along,' he said and pushed me towards the door.

I entered and locked the door behind me. From behind the door his brother said to me: 'The french letter's on the desk.'

I lit a cigarette and offered her one. She was sitting on the bed in her underclothes. She was wearing a

The Smell of it

cheap vest with holes in it, pink-coloured as though it were a piece of white cloth that had been dipped in blood and then washed several times. Her legs were bare. On the desk lay her frock, carefully folded.

'I don't want to smoke,' she said. 'Let's get on with it.'

'Let's finish the cigarette first,' I said. 'What's your name?'

'I want to get it over with,' she said and she stretched out her hand to my leg and undid my trouser buttons.

Slowly I turned her hand away.

'Sleep with me tonight,' I said, 'and then leave in the morning'.

She laughed: 'Is that so?' She pulled me towards her and tried to kiss me. I turned my mouth away from her face, then got to my feet. I took off my trousers and underpants and took hold of the french letter and began putting it on. It tore. I looked around for another one on top of the desk but didn't find one.

'I'm clean,' said the girl.

I opened the door and called out to Hassan's brother. 'I want one,' I said and he gave me one from his pocket. I put it on and threw myself on to her. She tried to kiss me. I turned my face away. At last I got up and put on my clothes.

Taking her with them, the two of them left. I sat on. I lit a cigarette. Ramzi came and I told him I'd been unable to sleep with the girl and he made fun of me. He had managed to. He'd met a girl in the street and had gone home with her. He'd put out the light and had stayed with her for ten minutes. Then he'd given her twenty-five piastres. After that he'd scrutinized his

The Smell of it

face in the mirror and had found it was all red. He said that there was nothing that was worth anything. He left. After a while the policeman came. I turned out the light and went to sleep.

In the morning I went out and breakfasted on the street. I didn't buy the newspapers. I returned to my room. My sister said that my uncle had returned from Alexandria and that he was very ill and that I must go and see him. I went out and took the Metro to the station. I got off the Metro, crossed the square and then passed through the outer wall of the station. I found him standing on the platform. He appeared to be in a normal state of health, with his wife beside him carrying an umbrella. His children hurried off to get a taxi and they all got into it and told me to meet up with them at the house. I got on to the Metro, went to their house, and found him seated on a sofa wearing his pyjamas. His body looked smaller than before, as though it had shrunk. I observed his shoulders which had grown thinner inside his vest and his two small eyes that were all but hidden behind thick glasses. His pyjama trousers were stained with large yellow patches above the bulky pouch between his thighs. He said that everything had begun with a feverish shivering. They called in the doctor who said there was nothing whatsoever the matter. He said his temperature had gone up in the evening and he thought he was going to die and he sent for the doctor immediately, who came and said 'Eat boiled food and have a urine test.' My uncle said he'd carried out the doctor's orders for one day only and on the following day he'd said to them, 'I want a chicken.'

The Smell of it

We got up to eat and he set about the meat, devouring it greedily. 'Give me some of the liver,' he said.

I left them and went out. I took the Metro to my cousin's house. I told myself that I'd know the house from its blue windows. I recognized the house as soon as I entered the street and saw the blue windows. But when I drew near to it I discovered that they weren't blue at all as I'd imagined. The glass was ordinary and colourless and it was merely the light from the sky that sometimes gave it that blueness. The shutters were cracked and the front of the house was a dirty yellow colour. The garden gate was open and was leaning against the wall. The garden itself was neglected and the coloured paving stones on the paths had been dislodged in several places. I walked along the path leading to the front door. Dog's excreta lay beside the wall. My cousin opened the door to me. I didn't recognize her at first. Her hair was untidy and streaked with many grey strands. Her eyes were dead-looking and the skin of her face dark-brown. In the living-room I saw where the north room was. I walked into it and said to her:

'Where's the sewing-machine which you used to keep here?'

'Do you still remember?' she said.

Yes, I still do. That was in winter. It was after lunch. In the south room sat my father with my aunt behind the glass of the veranda, facing the Palace. I went to him and wanted to sit on his knees. However, he shoved me away from him, saying that I was no longer so young. I left the room and went off to the hallway and crossed it to my cousin's room. She was sitting in front of the sewing-machine. I sat watching her as she

41

The Smell of it

worked the machine with her foot. 'Can you imagine,' she said to me, 'the thread broke on the very first turn. The man who put this machine together was a real devil.' She bent over the machine after giving me a quick glance. I turned my gaze to the window, feeling my ears hot. I was still seeing her soft white face and the pale rouge on her cheeks as I gazed at the closed window. It was the pane only that was closed and behind it appeared the sky and through it there flooded the fading rays of the sun. Down below in the garden the rays of the sun were lighting up the black well-mouth. After a while the children would come along and I'd go down with them and we'd raise water with the pump. We'd steal flowers and shake the mango tree in vain. We'd run about the basement and the underground passages, and this time I'd hide from them in the furthermost room, which was opened up in Ramadan for the Sheikhs to recite the Koran in every night. When we left at night my aunt would see us off to the door and put on the staircase light, and we would go down its wide white steps, out along the pathway, passing along its coloured stone slabs. We would open the garden gate which creaked, shut it securely, and dart out to the wide, quiet, soundless street. It was then that I would gather jasmine from the garden walls ... My cousin's friend said something. She was standing nearby in front of the wardrobe mirror and she was applying her lipstick. But I didn't look in her direction. She was tall and her eyes were green. She only addressed a single word to me: 'Hello', which she uttered on entering the room. Then she directed all her attention to my cousin. But my cousin was talking to me when she said, 'Just imagine.' Her small wardrobe was behind me, with two mirrors standing above its wooden panels, like two eyes. From the middle of it there hung down, from the key-hole, a small brass knocker that made a

The Smell of it

beautiful tinkling sound when the wardrobe was opened. Inside the wardrobe were locked drawers in which were stacked my cousin's belongings. I used to have a feeling of relief that the wardrobe was locked. Without moving my eyes from the window I was able to see her fingers lightly touching the handle of the machine, the wheel revolving noisily. She was hunched up, following the movement of the cloth under the needle, her plait of hair having fallen on her breast. 'Are you ever going to finish?' her friend said to her; 'we're late.' My cousin raised her head. Her eyes met mine as she looked at her friend. 'All right, the last row,' and I closed my eyes. After a while I heard the tinkling of the little brass knocker.

My sister came in and said: 'The sewers in the town are overflowing.'

An old relative of my cousin's entered. He was puffing badly. He couldn't see well from behind his spectacles. My cousin's face took on a glum look.

'Give me five piastres after I've drunk my coffee,' said the old man.

He took off his tarboosh and put it beside him on the sofa. He drank the coffee and sat on. My cousin went into her room, returned, and asked me if I had any change. I didn't have any. They sent the cook to change ten piastres into two fives. We sat waiting in silence until he returned. My aunt gave the five piastres to the old man, who rose, put on his tarboosh, said good-bye to us, and left.

'That old man's crafty,' said my cousin. 'He only puffs when he comes to our place.'

My sister said that he lived with his married son and that his son's wife egged her children on to rip up his

The Smell of it

clothes and hide his shoes, also that she left his room dirty.

'He'll drink the five piastres,' said my cousin.

'When he goes to his daughter's,' said my sister, 'she leaves him in the hallway and goes and locks herself in her room.'

'He spends the whole day out of the house,' said my cousin, 'drinking and calling on his relatives to beg.'

In this same hallway long years ago my aunt used to sit on the sofa in her white headcloth and smoke. At her side was my father, still panting from the stairs and the heat as he mopped at his bald head with its fringe of white hair. The cook came and my aunt took out her purse and gave him a pound. The cook left. My father said something to her and she shook her head. My father got up and crossed the hallway to the south room and went out on to the veranda. He lit his black cigarette and, leaning his elbow against the veranda ledge, began to smoke.

My sister said that Nihad had become engaged to a director in the Public Sector. I related to my cousin how a relative of Nihad's had asked me if I was the son of the man with bristling moustaches. We laughed. My sister said that Nihad's grandmother was ill and that they couldn't bear her.

'Before my mother died,' said my cousin, 'she was bedridden for months and used to wet her bed.'

My sister said that my cousin's wife had had a miscarriage in the sixth month.

'That was the best thing that could have happened to her,' I said.

My sister was angry and accused me of being callous. She said I was the only person who would be unable to attend her marriage because of its being at night. She

The Smell of it

said that her girl friend Husniyya would get married a week later and that her uncle would return to his house. She said that her uncle used to live with her all the time after he had left his wife. She said that his wife never wore anything but black and that he used to say that all her underclothes were black. My cousin's dog approached me, shaking its head about. I stretched out my hand to stroke it, at which it lay down on its back and immediately a stream of urine flowed from it on to the floor. They said he'd become like this of late, no sooner lying on his back than he urinated.

I went off to my room and undressed. I prepared a cup of tea and sat reading a book about Van Gogh. I must have dropped off to sleep. I dreamt that I met up with my father. He looked tired. He sat squat-legged and glum on his bed. I didn't know what to say to him as it was a long time since I had last tried to see him. He had been around the whole of the time but I hadn't thought of going to him. Suddenly I awoke to the sound of the door-bell. I got up to answer it. It was the policeman. I went back in to get the book and he signed and left. I returned to my room, turned out the light, lit a cigarette, and stretched out on the bed, thinking about my father.

That was at night. My father was screaming with pain. I wanted to go to sleep. When they took him to the hospital I remained on alone at home. I was happy. When I went to see him I was shocked at his eyes. The irises were large and full of fear. He asked me why I was late. He never talked to me after that. 'Read to me,' he said. I sat beside him on a chair. He turned his back to me. I took up a magazine and read to him. After a while I bent over him in order to see his eyes. They

The Smell of it

were closed. I stopped reading. He opened his eyes, however, and said: 'I haven't finished yet.' I went on reading and began to be conscious of having a headache. After a while I stopped. He opened his eyes and I went on reading. At last he said: 'That'll do, you can go.' I left hurriedly, breathing a sigh of relief. After this he never asked anything of me. I didn't see the terror that was in his eyes. When they brought him back home they carried him from the car to his bed. In my brother's house they changed the chair coverings for dark-coloured ones and I didn't understand why. When he coughed up blood my brother went down to look for a basin and came back puffing and blowing. 'I went all over the place,' he said. He threw himself down on the sofa, panting as he gazed at us. In the end my father was laid out straight on his back and they covered his whole body and face with a white sheet and arranged his hands at the side of his body. They said he had not asked about me. I raised the sheet from his face but his eyes were closed.

I slept. In the morning I went to the new flat my sister was moving into that evening. The whole house was new and work was still being carried out on some of the floors. I found the door of the flat open and my sister's fiancé standing in front of it. He accompanied me inside and we crossed the hallway to the lounge and he showed me a large picture on the wall of a European-type house on a sea-shore with a boat in front of it.

'It's painted by my brother,' he said with pride.

Then we moved into the bedroom. We opened all four doors of the wardrobe. We sat on the bed and bounced on it, we felt its coverlets and pillows. We went out into the hall, opened the refrigerator and closed it again. He led me up to the door, indicated a

The Smell of it

light above it and said, 'Directly I open the door this light goes on automatically, then puts itself out when I close it.'

'Wait for me here,' he said, 'while I go and bring the heater and the stove.'

He went out and I seated myself in the dark hallway and lit a cigarette. I got up and pressed the light switch but the electricity hadn't been connected yet. I stared at the lamp-shade which was in the shape of a satellite. Again I seated myself at the table and began smoking as I regarded the shining arms of the chairs, without a scratch on them. After a while the heater arrived, but my sister's fiancé didn't come. I waited for him for a little longer while I smoked. I got up and went over to the window. I found that the sun was setting. Then I saw him walking along the street on his own in the direction of the house. There was no one else in the street. After a little while he came up. I shook him by the hand and said: 'Congratulations.'

I left the house and went back to my room. I turned on the light. I put the police book in my pocket. I sat down in a chair with my back to the door. I took up a book. After a while I got up and turned the chair round so that I faced the door. I went on with my reading. A moment later I glanced at the door from over the top of the book: the flat was immersed in darkness. To no avail I tried to go on reading. I got up and went out to the hallway. I turned on the light there. My neighbour's room was in darkness. I moved into the kitchen where I lit the lamp.

I returned to my room and once again took up the book. Suddenly there was a knock at the door. I got up

The Smell of it

to answer it. I remembered my sister saying that whenever there was a knock at the door she felt as though someone was going to come in and beat her up. To begin with I opened the peep window of the door and found the policeman in front of me. I opened the door to him. I took the book from my pocket and handed it to him. He signed and left.

I returned to my room. I tried to start reading again but wasn't able to. I began walking about the room. I stood at the window. All the windows in front of me were closed. I undressed and put on my pyjamas, then I locked the door of my room, leaving the light on in the hallway and the kitchen. I lit a cigarette and lay down on the bed. When the cigarette was finished I threw it out of the window. I turned my face to the wall and went to sleep.

Suddenly I awoke, conscious of having a bad headache and feeling very thirsty. I got out of bed. The night was not yet over. I opened the door and went to the bathroom. I leant over the tap and drank. Then I turned off the tap. I discovered that the floor of the bathroom was swimming in water. I returned to my room; there was a banana on the desk so I picked it up, peeled it and ate it, putting the skin back on to the desk. I returned to my bed.

Once again I woke up. Sunshine filled the room. I remained stretched out. I got up and taking the toothbrush and soap, went to the bathroom. I found that the whole floor was covered with water, which had made its way into the hall. The tap had gone wrong. Standing in the middle of the water, I washed my face and cleaned my teeth, then returned to my room,

The Smell of it

leaving my wet footprints all over the place. I dressed and left the room, locking it after me. I put out the light in the kitchen and hallway.

I left the flat and went down into the street. I took the Metro as far as it went. I walked along the Corniche by the Nile. I crossed the bridge and entered the first riverside café I came to. I chose a secluded table overlooking the river and sat down. The waiter came and I ordered coffee. I began gazing down at the waters in front of me. I followed with my eyes a boat in which a bare-chested young man was rowing. Suddenly one of the oars slipped from his grasp and was taken away by the waters. The young man turned the boat's rudder in an attempt to catch up with the lost oar. Now he was rowing with one oar, every few seconds transferring it from one side of the boat to the other. But the water was flowing against him, and as each time he almost succeeded in reaching his goal, it eluded him. He began rowing with frenzied strokes. He looked desperate. Suddenly he let go of the one oar, cupped his hands to his mouth and shouted out to a companion of his in a faraway boat, seeking his help. But his companion did not reply, perhaps did not hear him.

My coffee hadn't come. I called out to the waiter, who didn't pay me any attention. I got up and left the café. I walked to the bridge and boarded a bus. I got off at the beginning of Soliman Street. I sat down in the first café I came to. I drank a coffee, then lit a cigarette. I got up and walked to Tewfik Street, then I branched off into Tewfikiyya and stood in front of the Cairo Cinema. It was showing a comedy. I went off in the direction of Fouad Street, which I crossed. I turned

The Smell of it

down into Sherif Street. I continued walking, crossed Adly Street, then Sarwat Street, and went off in the direction of Soliman Street, and continued on until I reached the Square. Water from the sewers overflowed the street. Pumps were set up everywhere, pumping the water out from the shops into the street. The smell was unbearable. I met someone I knew. He said he too had woken up only an hour ago. He was walking at a brisk pace so as to be in time for an appointment. I hurried along beside him and said: 'I'll walk with you to your appointment.' However, he said, 'We must part now,' and left me.

I crossed the street and went back in the direction of the Square, then I plunged down into Kasr El-Nil Street until I reached the cinema there. I looked at the advertisement saying that this world was a mad world. I moved to the ticket window: it was a full house. I found the advance booking window, but it was fully booked for both evening performances. People were booking for tomorrow and even further ahead.

I left the cinema and once again walked in the direction of the Square, and back into Soliman Street. This time I walked on the opposite side to the one I had come by. When I reached the Metro Cinema I found that it too was showing a comedy. I passed by it. I stood in front of the Americaine Café, undecided. The Rivoli Cinema was on my left and there was a vast crowd in front of it. The cinemas of Emad El-Din Street came to my mind. I crossed the street and continued walking up Fouad Street to Emad El-Din; I turned into it, walking on the left-hand side. There were

The Smell of it

enormous crowds at all the cinemas, though they didn't begin for another hour and a half.

I continued on to the end of the street. I cut into Ramses Street and made off in the direction of Bab El-Hadid Square. For a moment I had the impression I was being followed; I may have been mistaken. Then I checked my watch with the station clock and made my way to a café in the Square at the beginning of Republic Street, where I sat outside. Suddenly the sun disappeared and greyness reigned. I remembered this district from twenty years ago – the smoke from the trains inside the main station and the greyness everywhere – in the sky, the streets, and the houses.

I told myself that I should get up and search around for the old house. Perhaps my mother was still there. I quickly got to my feet before the sun came back. I wanted to make my approach to the house in overcast weather. I crossed Clot Bey Street. I left Faggala Street and cut across the small streets connecting it with the Square. I felt that I was approaching the place where the house was, and that by cutting across several side streets I would get near to it. I decided, however, to approach it from the direction of Faggala Street as we used to do, my father and I.

We would come by tram. We'd take it from the Square before it turned off into Zahir Street. I used to love this quiet street because it was full of trees whose dense branches used to meet high across the middle of it, shutting out the light. I used to love the sound of the trolley-arm thrusting its way with difficulty between the branches overhead. Even so the tram would charge down this street at top speed and we would give our faces to the noon wind and my father would put his hand on his

The Smell of it

tarboosh to stop it flying off. At the end of the street the tram would once again turn off into Mosque Square, would slow down and then come to a stop in front of the mosque. I would look out from the other side at its large garden that sloped downwards until it disappeared from the view of those sitting in the tram. From between its large domes I would see the children, brightly dressed, playing in the garden. My eyes would remain on them as the tram continued on its way, circling round the mosque until it, together with its garden, all at once disappeared. Once again the tram would turn to take us across narrow Khalig Street. I used to wish that the tram we were on was the Khalig one, so that we might pass between the two sides of the street which were so close together that my father, stretching out his hand from the window, could almost touch the walls of the houses. At last we would get off in Faggala. My father would take me by the right hand and we would cross the street, then go down another narrow one and walk along beside a high white wall over which hung the boughs of trees. Suddenly the street would go dark, then as quickly the darkness would lift. When I looked upwards I could see thick smoke quickly massing above us, which would be presently dispersed. My father said it was the smoke of trains coming from Bab El-Hadid station. The street came to an end, then the house we were going to made its appearance. My father would sit waiting on the doorman's chair while I climbed the steep stairway, passing by doors from which issued the smell of fat frying. After that my father and I would again go across the narrow street to alongside the white wall. It was then that I would catch sight of the enormous bells behind it. Over the street darkness reigned and it would appear empty of people. At the end of it a large blob of light could be seen which, as we approached, would reveal itself to be a cigarette shop. We

The Smell of it

would stand in the entrance, which had been blocked off by a large, high show-case. I would glue my face to the glass which in parts had become opaque. I would gaze at the packets of sweets and chocolate. By my head I would see my father's hand stretching out to the top pocket of his trousers to take out some money to roll over the glass right above my head. Then we'd leave the shop and cross the street to the tram stop. I would feel cold and stick closely to my father, and he would turn up the collar of his coat so as to cover his chest. We would stand at the stop. The street would have become deserted, the two of us standing alone in the middle of it. Then the tram would come and we'd get into the open carriage at the back. I'd huddle up in a corner and the tram would set off with us on the return journey. We'd pass through Khalig Street, then turn to the right. Ahead of us would stretch a vast dark void into which I was frightened to fall and I'd cling on to my father, and he would catch hold of my bare knee with his warm hand. After a while my eyes would grow accustomed to the darkness and I would make out the large square, the mosque a mass of darkness in the middle of it. The tram would pass round the mosque and we would leave behind us a closed-down cinema to which we used to go with my mother in the summer. Then we'd plunge into tree-filled Zahir Street. I'd rest my head against the wooden partition at the rear so as to enjoy to the full the extraordinary speed of the tram and I'd catch sight of my father closing his eyes against the wind that violently assailed us.

I followed the tramline up to the church and entered the street alongside it. It was crowded and full of noise. The street came to an end. I turned to the right. The house I remembered was very high and had wide wooden balconies, from one of which my mother once threw herself and fell on the balcony below. I ran my

The Smell of it

eye over the houses. They were all low. Only one had balconies made of wood. I told myself that this must be the one. I slowly approached it. The balconies were small and the entrance narrow. The entrance I remembered was a wide one. I passed through the entrance and slowly mounted the stairway. The stairs ended sooner than I had expected. At the very top was a small room. I knocked on the door. I heard a female voice say, 'Come in.'

I pushed open the door and stood in the entrance. There were three women garbed in black squatting on a bed in the corner. One of them got up and hurried towards me, saying: 'Who is it?'

I recognized in her my grandmother. I told her my name in a low voice. She hugged me and kissed me on the cheek.

'Sit down,' she said.

I sat down on a wooden seat in the entrance to the room.

'This is your aunt,' said my grandmother, indicating the younger of the two women.

My aunt came up to me and kissed me on the cheek.

'This is *my* aunt,' said my grandmother and she indicated the other woman. I got up and carried the chair over to be near them, then placed it by the bed and sat down.

'It's a small world,' said my grandmother's aunt.

'The moment I saw you I sensed it was you,' said my grandmother.

'We were only just saying we might meet one of them in the bus without knowing them,' said my aunt.

My grandmother took up the transistor radio and

The Smell of it

said: 'It's time for the play.' A solemn voice on the radio announced one of *The Black Ghost* episodes.

The episode started with a young boy asking in a tearful voice how he could go on living after knowing that his father was the murderer. I sat listening in silence. Their eyes were all glued to the radio. Half an hour went by and the play came to an end. My grandmother got up to perform her prayers. Several small children came along and my aunt said to them:

'This is the son of your aunt, God rest her soul.'

She glanced sideways at me.

I didn't speak. I now wanted to know exactly when and where my mother had died. My grandmother finished her prayers and came and sat beside me.

'When exactly did my mother die?' I said to her.

'Tomorrow will make it just a week ago,' she said.

'Where?' I said.

'At her father's,' she said.

I pointed to my head. 'And how was she?' I said.

'She was reading the newspapers,' said my grandmother's aunt, 'and talking about everything better than us, predicting everything that would happen, and she didn't get upset.'

'Then suddenly she became ill,' said my grandmother, 'and refused to see the doctor or to take any medicine. Gradually she got thinner and thinner and then she gave up eating altogether.'

'On the final day,' said my aunt, 'she asked for a glass of water and when she had drunk it she fell down dead.'

We were silent.

'Right up to the last moment,' said my grandmother, 'she didn't want to see either you or me.'

The Smell of it

I looked at my watch. It was getting near to the time for my appointment with the policeman. I got to my feet.

'I must go now,' I said.

I said good-bye to them and went down the stairs and out of the house. I crossed the side roads until I came to Ramses Square, then I turned off in the direction of the Metro tram stop.

The Snake

الثعبان

The Snake

And so the road suddenly made its appearance. It was when the driver slowed the car down, bending apprehensively over the steering-wheel, and continuing to take it up the steep slope, then following the road round as he gave several sharp hoots. There was not a sign of a living creature for tens of kilometres in every direction. No one could expect otherwise in this vast and remote desert, yet the driver had to be on the look-out for the unexpected at every bend or rise.

The doctor held his breath as he gazed out of the window at the rocks, huge as fortresses, that stuck up on every side. The noise inside the car grew less, and died away as all the passengers leaned against the windows, staring out in terror at the vast abyss that fell away right alongside the road. At the bend the car slowed down further until it was almost at a standstill. It continued forward at a crawl. There were several short wooden posts painted in red and black fixed along the edge giving warning of the chasm. Two of these posts were lying on the ground. The car negotiated the bend and the road sloped away in front

The Smell of it

of the driver, who straightened himself in his seat and let the car creep down without altering speed. There was another bend and again the road turned upwards. The sun shimmered on the huge rocks and their black masses gave one an uneasy feeling.

The doctor turned his head round in order to look at the section of road they had left behind them. Below, the long narrow road stretched out amidst the desert in an endless black ribbon, twisting back on itself, falling and rising in circles. He felt the breath of the passenger sitting behind him striking against the back of his neck in short, successive bursts. Then he heard him mutter in a low voice: 'Eh, it's like a snake.'

It was then that everything began to look like something else. Before that there had been nothing but irritation at the four hours the journey would take to Assiout. At the beginning the road had stretched straight ahead, with the desert spread out to left and right unendingly, no single rise obstructing it. The mountains were no more than faraway lines on the horizon. There was nothing to suggest that the geography of the place would change, for the journey coming had been by night, which had hidden the details of the road, its true nature being revealed only when it began to twist and turn up and down, bending and winding as it thrust snake-like forwards.

No bird, animal, or human was to be seen anywhere. There was nothing but sand and rock, also the posts that followed each other in fleeting succession on the sides of the road, some bearing instructions to the driver, others various numbers, of which the doctor failed to distinguish between those specifying the

The Snake

distance still remaining to Assiout from those indicating the distance already traversed by the car. Another group of objects was more like small tombstones bearing numbers that had been effaced and which resembled the old stone busts of Greek and Roman philosophers, pictures of which appeared in books and magazines.

To the left the poles for the telephone that linked the Oases with Assiout ran with the car. Sometimes the poles were supported by wires fixed into the ground, which in turn were made fast with a blocking of stones so that the violent desert winds should not sweep them away. Sometimes the posts stood erect independent of any wires or fixed only by a solitary wire. The poles were thin trunks of brown wood with a short cross-bar at the top so that they looked like crosses. Hundreds, or rather thousands, of these poles raced past the doctor in a straight line on the left. To him they were more like crosses that had been got ready for refractory rebels to be fastened to. Each to be fastened by the hands, the arms to be affixed to the cross-bar, and a long nail driven into the palm of each hand; the body to be tied to the pole with thick cord so that all the weight should not fall on the hands. Blood would ooze from the hands, from the nose, and the mouth. A putrid smell, that drew to it the flies, the vultures, and the wolves would be given out, and the head would loll in dwindling impotence. The eyes, closed yet fluttering from time to time, would give out a bewildered look in whose depths would be accumulated hidden powers that strove to ascertain or comprehend something or other. Perhaps the lips would move too and flutter like

The Smell of it

the eyes. But no one would ever know what their owner wanted to say.

Somewhere the doctor had read about the crosses set up by the Romans on one of the roads leading into Rome two thousand years ago and on which they had suspended the bodies of six thousand slaves. Those were slaves who had rebelled, had fought, and been defeated. Their crucified bodies remained for some time a source of pleasure and enjoyment to the free Romans. As for the crosses, it seemed their appetite for blood had remained unappeased ever since: the Romans had taken them to their colonies and even after they themselves had left, others had adopted them. It occurred to the doctor that the crosses had no doubt been placed close together like these poles, and that there were still people who enjoyed the sight of blood and crucifixion. Also there were still slaves who rebelled, fought, and were defeated: like the men who were brought to him when he was a doctor in the prison. They stood in front of him in silence, their heads lowered, their chests and backs bared so that their wounds showed, as though they had just been brought down from off the crosses before the birds of prey should tear them to pieces.

The crosses were racing the car. They put on speed when it did, slowed down as it slowed down. The wires that connected them shook from time to time when the winds blew. But the air had become close. The sun glowed and the driver began to slow down slightly. He was sitting quietly, paying no attention to anything around him. He must inevitably have had a feeling of awful boredom, for what pleasure could there be in

The Snake

going back and forth along this long road where there was no relief from the monotony of the scenery? The telephone poles were the very same: the rocks; the kilometre signs; the two empty resthouses; the lorry halted by the side of the road with its driver curled up asleep on top of it; that solitary tent.

It held no trace of life. It was as though its occupants had suddenly deserted it for some reason, or as though wild beasts had preyed upon them, leaving nothing of them. However, somebody appeared suddenly in the doorway of the tent when the car approached it. He was dressed in soldier's uniform and wore a beret on his head, which he pushed back, and drops of sweat appeared on his face and neck. He opened his tunic, revealing a dirty vest. Carrying a small notebook in his hand, he slowly approached the car, which had come to a complete stop. He moved towards the driver's door, his features puckered with annoyance.

The doctor realized that it was a control point. At the doorway of the tent another soldier, carrying a gun in his hand and wearing nothing on his feet, appeared. He stood looking at the car without interest, letting his eyes wander over the windows, doubtless in search of some woman's face with which to moisten the aridity of the desert. The doctor reckoned that there was no one but these two soldiers here. He tried to imagine how they spent their time throughout the long days and nights, and how the two of them got their food. It occurred to him that inevitably they must suffer during the night, for the cold of the desert is as unbearable as its heat. Inevitably, too, they must sleep close together. Perhaps, one night, feeling cold and

The Smell of it

lonely, one of them would cling closely to his companion. For at night – when the cold is intense and the scant coverings are incapable of combating it, and when the sky seems formidable and silent, and the wolves and the wild beasts no one sees are howling – then you know not what may happen.

The doctor was able to perceive the sensation of cold and loneliness in any human being. Maybe the reason for this was that he had spent a large portion of his working life in prisons. In these dark buildings – yellow from outside, murky within – you see everything as normal. When the prisoners used to come to his room for him to examine them, he would regard them with curiosity. They were extremely miserable: sick, aged, and broken. He could not distinguish between them because of their similar blue clothing and expressions of indifference. Some were really sick and had suffered much before reaching him. The others would mobilize all the cunning and guile they possessed to obtain from him a glass of milk, a piece of meat, or a blanket. Yet the doctor could see fear and pain in all their faces.

At the beginning – when he was a young man full of vigour, when everything used to look clear and simple, as the road did this morning before it twisted and turned and tied itself into knots like a snake – he used to think he'd be able to conquer pain. But he was deluding himself, for pain was like cancer – you tear it up by the roots in one place and it immediately makes its appearance in another.

He had reached the point where he used to wake up screaming every night after a dream that never varied.

The Snake

In this dream he would see himself sitting at a small table, his stethoscope hanging round his neck, and behind him a prisoner carrying a container with some red liquid in it which he knew to be blood. After each examination he would immerse his fingers in this container. On both sides of him stood two giants, like guards, in the white garb of nurses: he was dwarfed by them. In front of him were rows of prisoners seated on the ground, but they were not looking at him. Their gaze was directed at one of the giants, who was chewing something between his teeth, while his eyes roved round vacantly and his features looked angry and fierce, giving warning that at any moment he might ragingly return to consciousness. The fat contractor would bring in the milk – which would be drunk by those prisoners who were ill – for the doctor to test it. The man would put the container of milk in front of him on the ground, then pour into it a bucket of dirty washing water. Then another man would enter carrying the carcass of meat from which the prisoners would eat; he would approach him so that he could test it; smilingly he would show him its diseased and lacerated parts, and would then take it off inside. As for him, he would wave his hands and want to shout, protest, refuse, and threaten, but the sound would be imprisoned in his throat and there it would grope about, clawing with its talons at the roof of his mouth.

But it was not possible for this to go on for ever; it was destroying his nerves.

His nerves were calm now. His stomach, though, had begun to be upset by the bumping of the car. For,

The Smell of it

despite the fact that the road had been built and made up two years ago, the paving had been damaged in many places. The doctor thought that the opening up of the road could not have been a difficult matter, for the desert stretched out like a plain except for one or two places. The car was now approaching one of these uneven places, which was a semi-tunnel in the middle of a mountain on which could be seen the marks of recent work. There was no doubt that hands and machines had cleared this tunnel in the middle of the mountain. The two feet of the mountain, with their red rocks, were very close together. The car proceeded slowly through the tunnel and the whole air became dyed red. The driver again bent over the steering-wheel apprehensively, and the passengers looked out of the windows in terror at the huge rocks suspended over the mountain foot an arm's distance away, as though about to fall at any moment.

The doctor was gazing with curious anticipation at the mountain peak and base as though expecting coloured heads to emerge from them, shrieking, assailing them like locusts, and raining down poisoned arrows upon them as happened in films. Or that shots would suddenly ring out from everywhere, aimed by unknown enemies lying in ambush. It did not occur to the doctor that he was dreaming or imagining things, for he knew that something similar was happening on the other side of the desert across the sea. Perhaps at this very moment there was just such a mountain over there, with red rocks and ravines and caves in which the killers were hiding. Perhaps there was a soldier sitting on the edge of it, while behind him several

The Snake

half-naked men, carrying daggers and knowing nothing about anything except killing, were stealing up upon him. Silently they would fall upon the soldier and stab him all over. He would roll to the ground, his blood leaving a red line behind him: quickly it would congeal, coagulating with the earth. He would roll rapidly, the dust rising above him, until he came to rest at the bottom. Above, the brutish fighting would continue, then stop after victory had been achieved. Reconstruction would begin. Roads would be opened, factories would be built, cinemas put up, and love songs would be composed and broadcast over the radio. The murdered soldier would not hear them. He would see none of all this, for he would never again leave his place in the desert.

In the desert the doctor was travelling on in the car, irritated by the heat and the boredom. His watch told him that the car had covered half the distance. He was thinking that he should have brought a small radio with him to while away the journey. In Cairo people were eating ice-cream and drinking glasses of iced mango juice and watching the television. Again they passed by a lorry that had turned off on to the side of the road, its driver curled up on the back of it fast asleep.

In front of him in the car were sitting two smart young men, one of whom expressed the opinion that the road stretching before them through the sands reminded him of the road to Alexandria. This also was the view of the other who had had some strange experiences on that road when he was going along it in a small car called *Kiki*. Beside the door was sitting a

The Smell of it

passenger of slender build, huddled in his seat which was over the raised part above the front mudguard, looking dwarfed. He was immersed in his thoughts, as though reckoning up his life. Certainly his thoughts were not heartening. This was not surprising, for when one is in the middle of the desert and one's face is pouring with sweat and the road in front appears to have no end, when thigh muscles ache and nerves have begun to protest, when one is squirming about in one's seat searching for somewhere to be comfortable, when, besides, one has passed forty – then death becomes embodied before one as the finality of everything.

To any doctor death is something familiar, although it sometimes causes one to reflect about it. This was what had happened yesterday: when he was making his tour of the hospital wards in the Oases, depressed by the flies, the heat, and the dust, he had been thinking that death was the fate of everyone, and that no ill person was the worse off if he should die today rather than tomorrow seeing that this was bound to happen one day. This thought was a simple and intriguing one. It meant that he should finish this disagreeable task quickly in order to take himself off to the Governor's air-conditioned room.

This was an easy matter; during the last few years it had been without any importance to him. It was enough to keep the inside of one cold and unmoved in order not to care, for everything to appear plain and easy, and for things to carry on uncomplicatedly. The floor was filthy, the pails of water that had been poured over it hastily to remove the filth having been unsuccessful. The male nurses were clothed in sparkling

The Snake

white uniforms, but he knew they would take them off when he turned his back on them. The sheets covering the beds were clean, but he was able to imagine what was hidden beneath them. Yet all that was of no importance. It was enough that everything appeared all right and that he was able to make his departure immediately.

The sick lay on their beds in clothes that were identical and approximated in colouring to the yellowness of their faces. They were following him with their eyes, but for which he would have supposed them to be corpses devoid of life. From the way they looked at him he realized that he should not give any one of them an opening or he would never get finished. And so he kept to the wing of the main corridor between the beds and avoided meeting the eyes of any of them. He would turn his back on them, raise his eyes to the ceiling, put his hands in his pockets, and incline his head forward so as to gaze at some object on the bare stone floor. But always he felt the eyes fixing themselves upon him: strong and commanding, drawing him despite himself. They would compel him to turn to them, to face them perplexed. The sockets were wide and deep-set, but something strange was gathering itself together in their depths; something that drew and bound and fettered; something ancient and familiar that could not be ignored.

*   *   *

The doctor relaxed in his seat and continued to look out of the window opposite, by the left-hand pane of

The Smell of it

which sat the driver. He knew that the snake stretched out behind. In front there was nothing. The road did not appear to extend beyond a few paces ahead. The desert concealed it carefully, only revealing it bit by bit. The road would sometimes rise up suddenly, and only a single step ahead was to be seen. The driver would press down on his horn in warning, and when the rise vanished the road would unroll ahead again, completely featureless. The doctor almost smiled at the deception that was incessantly repeated and which each time tricked him. To the rear, the snake could be clearly seen twisting away, leaving its tail far away, way back at the Oasis. As for the head, it was creeping forward with feverish speed, craning its neck in yearning impatience to see what was to come. Suddenly the mountains appeared, as though barricading the road. For a moment the doctor wondered where the driver would take himself, how he would get through. But the head of the snake soon pushed its way miraculously through at a place in the vicinity of the mountains.

The road was now free from bumps. The car was racing along quickly and easily. The kilometre number signs followed one another. The doctor was able to solve the puzzle of these numbers now and to tell which indicated the distance that remained and which showed what had been completed. The distance that remained to Assiout was no more than fifty kilometres. Silence reigned in the car. Some of the passengers leaned their heads forward on to the backs of the seats opposite them and had sunk into sleep.

The doctor's irritation had reached its peak. His eyes

The Snake

were tautly focused on the country that undulated through the other side of the window, and at every bend or rise he indulged the hope that after it would appear the houses and buildings of Assiout; but each time he was suddenly confronted by new hills and expanses of sand. The road looked endless. The kilometres seemed to get longer, to come to an end only with great effort – the number forty remaining static for a long time. Finally the doctor decided to refuse to have anything to do with these numbers and not to follow them with either his eyes or his mind, to think of something else with which to occupy the time. It was then that the long dark line appeared.

It stretched far away into the horizon, but was rapidly coming nearer. To begin with it most resembled a heavy cloud in the far sky, then it soon seemed nearer to the earth than to the sky. The doctor turned round slightly to the passenger sitting behind him and asked him his opinion. The latter immediately gave his reply – with a sigh of relief he said: 'Assiout'.

The car was now scarcely touching the ground. A kilometre sign passed and he saw it said thirty. The dark line began, moment by moment, to grow clearer and its dark colour turned to a dense green, which rapidly drew closer the head of the snake every moment tilting to right and to left with the turnings of the road as it resolutely made its way towards the greenness. The passengers began to lose their lassitude and to rise in their seats as they gazed with interest at the faraway fields. This was the moment when there appeared the large white slabs arranged in sloping rows opposite the fields. The doctor leaned forward as he

The Smell of it

followed them with his gaze, wondering what they were. After a while he discerned large stone structures, like benches, some of which consisted of several storeys, like the step pyramid of Sakkara. There were not so many of them. They were well-proportioned and the sides were of equal size, the edges polished – or this was how it appeared from afar. Some of them bore lines and naïve patterns in red, like those drawn on the houses of returning pilgrims in the villages or the poorer quarters of the towns, and on which they would scrawl: Pilgrim shriven, sin forgiven.

The doctor fidgeted in his place, perplexed. The passenger sitting behind him, as though conscious of his perplexity, said: 'This is Assiout's cemetery.'

A faint smile traced the doctor's lips, and it occurred to him that he had never seen graves such as these, though he had visited many villages and towns. The car turned to the left, having slowed down, and began to cross a steel bridge. Suddenly people appeared on every side as though the ground had spewed them forth. The peasants began, as was always their wont, to inspect the car and its occupants in astonishment. Three young schoolchildren hurried along the side of the bridge, their sleeves rolled up, hugging their books tightly to them. The doctor's gaze followed them with nostalgic sadness. The car crossed the bridge and turned off into a broad street shaded by trees. The Nile waters flowed along on the right, deep and vast.

The journey had not come to an end yet, for there still remained a few kilometres to the town. The snakelike road, however, had disappeared; when the doctor turned round to look he detected not a trace of it. By then it was buried in the sands of the desert. Likewise he could not make out the strange tombs of Assiout, for the tall, bulky, blue gum trees screened everything that lay behind them. The trunks of these trees had begun to take up the race with the car.

Arsène Lupin

أرسين لوبين

Arsène Lupin

I approached the shop hesitantly. When I was by the door I looked furtively inside and found what I had expected: the man was stretched out in an old chair, his galabiya exposing his huge muscular leg, as he breathed loudly. I stood by the door not knowing what to do. Before me, to the left, were the two small shelves which I had been dreaming of the whole of these past days, holding tens, even hundreds, of the thin pocket novels. Between them and me was but a pace or two. The man was asleep, but I was afraid he would wake up and see me. Yet, at the same time, I could not leave. I could not imagine myself being all day long without a novel. I stepped inside.

Placing my hand on his leg, I called his name. Immediately the sound of his breathing ceased. His body shook slightly, then his left eye opened out of a red circle, and his lips let forth a bellow.

Pointing to the novels I said to him: 'I'll look around for a novel.'

Another bellow issued from his mouth. It seemed to me that he would swoop down upon me and dash me to pieces. However, he sat up straight, sighing, and

The Smell of it

began wiping his neck with a dirty handkerchief. His bloodshot eyes, fully opened, stared out at me. I moved away from him. When he still said nothing, I slowly made my way to the two shelves and stood in front of them as I went through the novels.

The novels were old, their covers had disappeared and the pages were yellowed and torn. Dust rose out of them and was mingled with a strange smell which came from everything in the shop. I loved this smell.

I went through them quickly, making do with a glance at the first page in search of a line in small type under the title. I finished the first shelf without having found what I was looking for. I felt uncomfortable and the sweat began to pour down my face. I looked furtively at the man, fearing that he would burst out at me, but his bloodshot eyes continued to look at me in silence.

Suddenly he said: 'There's no Arsène Lupin.'

My hands paused in their work. There was still a whole shelf to go through. It seemed to me that he wanted to get rid of me. I decided to continue my search. Looking around with great haste, I was unable to find a single novel about Arsène Lupin. I overcame the oppressive feeling which had taken hold of me and went back to a leisurely search through the novels. I now wanted to find any ordinary detective novel.

The Flower of Death I had read. *The Complete Crime* my father had already brought home. *The Chinese Puzzle* was the first Arsène Lupin novel I had read. *The Three Eyes* by Maurice Leblanc: It was by the same author as the Arsène Lupin books but was not about him; I had already been 'had' by this. If only there was an Arsène

Arsène Lupin

Lupin novel which had escaped my notice in my first search! *Execution at Dawn* looked as though it were a tragedy, and I did not like gloomy novels. *Great Love* – I did not like romantic novels either. *The School of Secrets* – you couldn't tell what it was about from the look of it. *The Mask of Death*, *The Riddle of Riddles* – all these I had read. *The Wreckage* – its title and appearance were not encouraging.

I lowered my hand despairingly – my arm had begun to ache. It seemed that I would not be taking anything away with me this time.

The man, who was sitting behind me, bellowed: 'Is there nothing in all that lot that you like?'

I answered quickly, continuing my search: 'No – here's one.' *Crime Amidst the Clouds*; though I had already read it I might as well take it again seeing that I had not found anything else. I put it to one side. *Anonymous Letters* – I had read it. A novel called *The School of Secrets*; I thought I'd try it, perhaps it would prove the surprise of all time. *The White Sisters*, *Our Daily Bread*, *Eugène Grandet* – novels without meaning, each one of which could be a 'cheat'; what was certain was that none of them was a detective novel. There were no Sherlock Holmes books, or even Charlie Chan ones, though I found him quite insufferable. All the novels were short. If only I could find one of those large, old novels, if only I could by chance come across the novel we had had at home when I was very young and which, sadly, I had never read right through because at that time I did not read novels, and because some of its pages had been torn. However, what I had read of it was enough to strike terror in my breast and had

The Smell of it

made me tear it up in order to escape from it. I still remember a description of a shore and a deserted castle in which a crime took place and people were running about in the darkness and talking in whispers. There was also the novel *The Red Eye*. Then there was the novel my father was at present reading.

A sudden voice nearby me, in fact right over my head, rang out:

'Off with you! No novels – we're not selling novels.'

The man had jumped up from the chair, shaking with anger, and snatched from me the novels I had kept in my hand in order to choose some of them when finally I had failed to find some lovely novel, and I looked round in despair. All this searching only to return with nothing! I spotted a book with a thick black cover lying nearby. I quickly picked it up and opened it. Its pages were rough and yellow, its print poor; it was clearly an old book. It had neither title nor beginning, and quickly flipping through its pages, I realized it consisted of old detective stories.

Anxiously I said to the man: 'All right, I'll take this one.'

However, he snatched the book from my hand and gave me a push, shouting:

'We've got no novels – we're not selling novels.'

Sadly I moved away. I had no time to go to another shop. I had to return home immediately as my father did not know I had gone out.

When I entered the lane I walked close in to the walls, taking care that my father would not see me should he be standing on the balcony. I ran up the stairs so quickly that I was puffing and perspiring. I found the

Arsène Lupin

door of the flat ajar as I had left it, and crept inside, listening so as to define my father's whereabouts. Sensing that he was in the bedroom, I made my way to it and caught sight of him cross-legged on the edge of the bed with the wooden table in front of him on which he had placed his shaving box, which had originally been a cardboard carton of cigarettes, and the mirror leaning against a glass filled with water. He began honing the blade against the palm of his hand. I began watching the blade as it went back and forth, slowly and surely, across the firm flesh of his palm. I realized that he was going out. There was no indication he was aware of my having gone out. I sat myself down on a wooden stool in the corner and began watching him. He started lathering his chin, and then passing the razor across it as he leaned forward so as to see his face in the mirror. When he had finished, he rubbed his chin with a piece of alum so that it looked soft and fresh, and I felt I wanted to touch it with my fingers.

Suddenly he turned to me: 'Put on your clothes because you're coming out with me.'

To go out with him was better than ten novels. Perhaps along the way we would have the opportunity to buy a novel.

Before my sister realized what was happening and broke out crying and shouting and insisting on coming out with us, my father played a trick on her by saying to her that he would let her play the whole day in the flat of Umm Zakiyya, our neighbour.

My father put on his clothes and, smoothing out his tarboosh with the sleeve of his jacket, put it carefully on his head. We left the flat, locking the door behind

The Smell of it

us and hurried into the street. I noticed that we were making our way to the tram stop.

'Where are we going?' I asked him.

'You'll soon find out,' he answered.

We got on to the tram. We went a long way and finally got off in front of a large, walled building with crowds of people at the gate and in the courtyard.

'This is the court,' said my father. We went into the courtyard.

'Now we'll go inside,' said my father, 'and we'll find Mummy sitting with her mother.'

'Mummy?' I was amazed.

'Yes, you'll go and say hullo to her and see what she says to you.'

'And aren't you coming?'

'No, I'll wait for you outside in the corridor.'

My father led me into a larger, darkened hall. We passed by a door on the right. He pushed me towards it, saying: 'There she is, over there.'

I did in fact see her there.

She was sitting silently beside my grandmother. It was the latter who first caught sight of me. She gazed behind me intently, then a strange smile took shape on her lips, a smile I felt uneasy about, and she continued to look at me stiffly. Her face was framed in a faded white headcloth.

I approached her, looking at my mother. She was wearing a coat of black silk and had a coloured veil around her head, and I noticed too her long black hair. It seemed to me she had grown taller and broader since the last time I had seen her.

My mother saw me but gave no sign that she

Arsène Lupin

recognized me. Suddenly she addressed me quickly, just as though I had never been parted from her: 'How are you?'

But she did not ask me to sit down beside her. She turned away from me to contemplate what was going on in the hall. I stood up in confusion, not knowing what to do. I happened to glance into the outer vestibule and saw my father turn his head round in my direction as he walked up and down with his hands behind his back. I noticed there was an empty place beside my mother, so I sat down.

We were at the back of the hall, which was not crowded. It contained long benches, and at the end was a raised dais on which the cadi sat; on his left stood a sheikh in caftan, turban, and glasses, with a woman swathed in a black milaya; they were arguing.

This was the first time I had seen a court. I was amazed. I saw none of the things I had previously imagined: no heated pleading and crowded halls and a judge wearing a coloured sash and a lawyer waving his arms, his voice echoing out through the whole hall.

Suddenly my grandmother stood up. She went up to a man in a turban to whom she spoke for a while. I turned to my left and saw my father talking to several people. I glanced sideways at my mother and found she was still sitting gazing unconcernedly ahead of her.

My grandmother went off to the farthest end of the hall and talked for a while with the judge.

I noticed that my father was motioning to me from afar, so I stood up. I did not know what to say to my mother. She had not looked in my direction, so I went off without saying anything to her.

The Smell of it

My father said to me: 'So, what did she say to you?
'Nothing – she said "How are you?"'

My father and I went towards the door. We walked along the street which was narrow and had old shops on one side. My father was smoking. I noticed a shop that had some books in it. I pulled my father by the hand and said to him, as I prepared myself for a real battle: 'Daddy, let's ask about novels.'

My father made no objection. He accompanied me into the shop and asked the owner: 'Got any novels, old chap?'

The man produced five novels for us. I found that I had read them all except one. I almost jumped for joy, *Arsène Lupin at the Bottom of the Sea*. The novel was a new one with a coloured cover that was smooth and shining. I took the novel, and my father paid for it and we went out into the main street.

I now wanted to return home at top speed.

We got on to the tram and I put the novel on my lap, hiding its front cover. I began contemplating its back cover which was white and shiny and had an advertisement for the next novel to be published. The wind flipped up the last page and at the bottom of it I saw the delicious words written large 'The End'. I resisted reading the last lines of the novel and turned it over on to its front. It bore a large revolver with behind it the face of a man wearing a hat: it must be Arsène Lupin in person. The magical name was written in small letters at the base of the title. I read it several times, beside myself with happiness.

Across Three Beds in
the Afternoon

بَعَدَ الظُّهرِ عَبْرَ ثَلاثةِ أَسِرَّ

Across Three Beds in the Afternoon

He was hungry. The alarm clock placed above the television set pointed to eight o'clock. There were still twenty minutes to go before Sayyid returned, and then they would all start to eat.

He inclined his head slightly, listening to her moving about in the kitchen. He knew that she was now walking about energetically between the sink, the gas stove, and the table with the thin sheet-iron top, despite her sixty-five years, and that everything would be scattered round about her in utter confusion.

When she had almost finished she would call to him from the kitchen:

'Isn't it yet time for Sayyid to come back?'

He would look at the alarm clock, carefully examining it from behind his thick spectacles, and would then say to her:

'He must be on his way now.'

From the place he had chosen for himself on the bed he was able to see the door of the flat for when Sayyid would put his key into it, and with the familiar movement push against it to open it, and he would walk inside saying:

The Smell of it

'Peace be upon you.'

Despite the fact that his wife never stopped complaining that this position of his exposed him to draughts, he had continued to retain it ever since his recurrent illness had forced him to take to his bed, so that he might, as he put it, 'be in touch with events'. The room had three beds in it, two of which stood close to each side of the balcony door; the third joined up with one of them to make a straight line. When he lay down on it he was facing the balcony, and if he turned round and sat across the bed, leaning his back against the wall as was his wont, the door of the room was facing him, followed by the hallway, and then the front door of the flat.

Because of the draughts the balcony door was always kept closed night and day, summer and winter, so that those who visited them, in particular their daughter Fadia, always complained that the smell in the flat was unbearable.

According to the alarm clock Sayyid should now be at the top of the street, approaching with long, easy strides, the day's newspaper folded under his arm. On reaching the bread shop, he would stop and buy ten loaves, which he would wrap up in his newspaper, and then once again continue on his way to the Co-operative to see what new things they had on sale. If he were lucky ...

He sucked in his lips, hoping that Sayyid would bring with him some of those Ummahat dates which, besides being cheap, were easy to munch up and swallow, and had a sweet taste if dipped into white sesame oil; the latter, however, was not at present on the market.

He gave a characteristic shake of his head and, stretching out his fingers under his vest, he began scratching his chest violently to rub away the accumulated dirt. By reason of his illness he was excused from having a bath, a practice he had had no taste for since his youth, not so much through a dislike of cleanliness as through laziness. Thus, when young, he used to go to sleep in his outdoor clothes in order to save the time required for putting them on in the morning before going off to school – a habit he had been forced to abandon when he had taken his Primary examination and had joined the Ministry.

He interlaced his hands on his stomach and once again looked at the alarm clock. After ten minutes it would be time for the news bulletin. Sayyid would certainly come in before then and would turn on the radio which was placed in the hallway.

Before he was able to smell it, the spluttering sound of frying came to him from the kitchen. Seating himself up straight, he blinked behind his thick glasses as he strove to keep the front door of the flat in view so that he would not miss it being opened and Sayyid entering.

The mother's voice was raised from the kitchen:

'Sayyid? Have you come, darling?'

Having closed the door behind him, Sayyid crossed the hall. He put the bread on the dining-table, then moving to the room in the forefront of which his father was seated, said in a loud voice so that it might reach his mother as well:

The Smell of it

'Peace be upon you.'

The old man repressed his disappointment when he perceived that Sayyid had not brought any of the fruit with him; he stretched out his hand and took the newspaper from him, saying:

'What's the news?'

Sayyid pursed his lips as he seated himself on the edge of the bed beside his father, and put his fingers up to his tie to undo it.

'Nothing.'

Then casually:

'Just a military communiqué.'

Suddenly the old man became so animated that Sayyid added: 'Ten minutes' exchange of fire.'

'But war will break out,' said the old man, struggling against his feeling of disappointment.

Carrying his shoes in his hand, Sayyid looked round for his slippers. Not finding them, he called out:

'Mummy – where are my slippers?'

At forty-two Sayyid was still unable to remember where he left his various belongings before going out in the morning.

'You've got them, darling,' the mother answered from the kitchen. 'They're where you left them this morning.'

'Perhaps they're in your room,' said the old man, spreading out the newspaper and gazing at the headlines.

Barefoot, Sayyid went off to his room, where he found the slippers beside the door. He stood taking off the rest of his clothes in front of the large wardrobe mirror, which as usual reflected his face distorted.

Across Three Beds in the Afternoon

However, the softness of his skin and the lack of a trace of a single hair on his chin showed up on its surface. Were it not for a slight pallidity, somebody seeing him might mistakenly think he was in his twenties – and this would often occur.

He pulled open the flap of the wardrobe to put his clothes on the hanger, then he took up the pyjamas he had thrown on the chair that morning without folding them and began putting them on.

Sayyid used this room solely for the purpose of changing his clothes, and would spend all his time in the other room. When the mother had been ill for a long time, he had started to sleep in the third bed facing her, the bed which had belonged to his sister Fadia before she had married. Scarcely had the mother recovered than the father became ill, and thus Sayyid had stayed on in the third bed.

When he had finished putting on his pyjamas he heard his mother's voice from the kitchen:

'Sayyid. The plates, darling.'

He left the room. His father caught sight of him crossing the hall and called out:

'Put the radio on for Daddy.'

He went to the old radio and turned it on, waiting until it gave out a noise like the intermittent coughing of an old man; satisfied that the radio was working, he took himself off to the kitchen.

His mother was bent over the food on the stove. She turned to him and asked:

'Have you bought the cooking butter?' Several beads of sweat had collected above her conspicuous moustache.

The Smell of it

'There was a great crush at the door of the Co-operative,' said Sayyid, 'and I couldn't get in.'

He began collecting up the plates from the rack and carried them in to his father's room.

In the past they usually ate in the hall. Of late, however, they had, because of illness, come to eat in the same room as they slept, on a small table at the end of which the television was placed. The hall table was used only when guests came, which was rare now.

When Sayyid had brought the salt cellar, the spoons and knives, the mother appeared with her slightly bent back and flabby body, which shook as she moved to right and left. She was carrying a large bowl of potatoes cooked with tomatoes, which she placed in the middle of the table. Sayyid went to the kitchen and returned with a wide dish filled with rice.

The father made sniffing noises as he got out of bed with difficulty and took his place at the table. In comparison with the picture of him hanging on the wall he looked as though his body had shrunk to half its size.

'A glass of water for my medicine, Sayyid,' he said.

There was no need for him to have asked because Sayyid was, by force of habit, already in the process of bringing two glasses, not one, because both the father and the mother used to take a number of medicines, in the form of both pills and drops, before and after meals.

Breathing heavily, the mother filled a large plate with rice and potatoes to which she added salad, and gave it to her husband. She did it with the aplomb of someone performing an act that would go down in history. He

Across Three Beds in the Afternoon

started turning over and mixing up the food, then he attacked it with prodigious appetite, having forgotten about the news bulletin which the announcer was reading out in a grave voice. The mother piled up a similar plate for herself after having swallowed her medicine. As for Sayyid, he had started off with the potatoes on their own. There was no longer any sound except that of their mouths as they munched at the food, interspersed by the mother's heavy breathing.

'Hasn't Fadia phoned?' asked Sayyid.

'Not a word,' she said. Her preoccupation with the food prevented her from speaking at greater length, so she contented herself by adding: 'Perhaps she'll phone in the afternoon.'

The question and answer had been repeated at the same time for the last fortnight, for on that date Fadia had given birth to her first child. A month previously the mother had sworn that she wouldn't put a foot inside her daughter's house, while the girl's husband had likewise sworn that he would break her foot if she did so; thus neither the father, the mother, nor Sayyid had paid Fadia a visit when she had given birth, or afterwards. This had caused the husband to swear anew that he would divorce his wife were she to take her child to see its grandparents.

The mother and daughter, however, remained in touch by telephone. The latter would often place the receiver by her child's mouth so that his grandmother could hear his screaming or gurgling, although mostly he made no sound whatsoever.

The father having finished everything that was on his plate, the mother gave him another helping, which

The Smell of it

he attacked with the same gusto. The mother took the opportunity of a moment's break from eating to ask him:

'How does Daddy like the food?'

Ever since their marriage more than forty years ago they had been addressing each other as 'Daddy' and 'Mummy'.

'Bless you,' said the father through a full mouth, and several grains of rice fell on to his pyjama front.

The mother turned to Sayyid, who was eating with no less good an appetite than his father.

'Don't you yet know when your enquiry will take place?'

'No,' said Sayyid.

'It was in the power of the Head of the Department to finalize the matter himself without the need for an enquiry or anything of that sort,' she continued.

Sayyid shrugged his shoulders and did not reply.

Putting a large spoonful of the mixture of rice, potatoes, and salad into his mouth, the father asked: 'Was it necessary to change the universe?'

It was a comment that came as a surprise to Sayyid in that it was a harbinger of a change occurring in his father's attitude. Up until now he had believed that his father and mother were on his side, as they had always been. Were they not the only people who always gave him looks of admiration when, for instance, he announced to them the linguistic and grammatical mistakes he discovered in the newspapers, whereas at the firm he was met with looks of boredom and scorn, especially from Soleiman?

This was quite apart from the fact that he had no de-

Across Three Beds in the Afternoon

sire to change either the universe or anything else: all it amounted to was that he wanted to put matters right.

What, after all, was the sense of an Arab firm in an Arab country dating its letters to other Arab firms in figures rather than in letters?

'But Sayyid's right,' said the mother, looking at him with pride.

'What will we gain by writing the date in letters?' said the father whose faith in his son had been shaken by the prospect of the awaited enquiry.

Sayyid bent his head over his plate and began thinking about the matter despondently. Was there not a certain music pleasing to a trained ear about a sentence such as this: Written on the third of November of the year one thousand, nine hundred and sixty-nine? Or – the fourteenth of December of the year one thousand, nine hundred and sixty-eight. Ninety per cent of people today would not notice the difference in the grammatical inflections of the two sentences, brought about by the fact that in Arabic there are two words for 'year' of different genders. Are there many people capable of distinguishing the correct form in which to write 1912, for example, in letters, there being no less than four different ways of writing 'twelve'?

Had Soleiman not objected and taken the matter to the Head of the Department, no difficulty would have arisen. Many such matters occurred every day that were open to the sort of change Sayyid had wrought in the dating of letters, matters that would normally pass unnoticed. But Soleiman – someone without any subject of daily conversation except his innumerable amatory conquests – had wanted to make an issue of

The Smell of it

the matter, and an occasion for exhibiting his talent for ingratiating himself. What would the firm do when writing to other firms in Arab countries that used different names for the months? Would it date its letterswith two different words for the months, sometimes three?

Sayyid was at no loss for words to defend his views to the Head of the Department. Numbers are always liable to error, and for this reason cheques, for example, are written both in figures and words. There was also the basic argument that the figures used were alien to the Arabic language. Had the Head of the Department been somebody more serious-minded, the matter would have ended with his suggestion being accepted and that would have been the end of it.

The father had finished what was on his plate and had left his spoon balanced on the side of it. He sat back in his chair and placed his hand on his stomach.

A whole plateful of food took him no more than a few minutes to get through because, having lost all his teeth long ago, he masticated none of it.

'Shall I give you some more?' his wife asked.

'Thanks be to God, but I've had enough,' he said. He took two of the pills to be taken after meals and swallowed them with the rest of the water in his glass. Then, getting up from the chair, he went to the bed and stretched himself out on his back, interlocking his hands over his chest.

Lassitude had overcome him and he felt a strong desire for sleep. In a state of semi-doze he watched his wife and son as they removed the food that was left over and hurried off to their beds, their two heads placed in a line with his own. The three made a triangle

Across Three Beds in the Afternoon

with six eyes looking in one direction, which was the balcony door.

In the past a nap after lunch would last for a long time, after which the father would wake up refreshed and active. But in recent years it had become extremely short, so that he would soon wake up and remain stretched out looking at the ceiling without clearly distinguishing its details. Meanwhile, the sun outside would fall away on its path to its final disappearance, and the light in the room would gradually diminish. Then, raising his head from time to time, he would scrutinize the other two beds from behind his thick spectacles. Generally the mother too would wake up. What usually happened was that one of them would start up a conversation across the two beds at the time when the other had, in fact, just woken from sleep.

This conversation would usually begin by one of them – generally the father – mentioning that such-and-such a relative of his had not visited them for a long time. He would mention this in a matter-of-fact voice that outwardly suggested nothing. The other – generally the mother – would then do a swift calculation as to the last time this relative had visited them.

At which the father would say, pretending indifference: 'Perhaps he's too busy or he's ill – or it's somebody in his family. Who knows?'

The mother would immediately retort that this relative had been seen at so-and-so's last week, for, without leaving the house, she was fully informed via the telephone about what was going on in their small world.

This being the reply the father was awaiting, he

The Smell of it

would give a sigh. The conversation would then take one of two courses: either a review of all the information available about the personal life of this relative, or an enumeration of the other relatives and friends who had also not done their duty for some time by visiting them.

Today, however, the conversation took a different turn by reason of the fact that Fadia had announced over the telephone yesterday that her husband had got himself a contract to work in Kuwait and that they'd be going away just as soon as the child's health permitted.

'I'll die without seeing the boy,' said the father in his usual matter-of-fact voice.

His wife immediately answered: 'Don't say such a thing.' Then:

'May God take vengeance on whoever may be the cause!' little knowing that she was exposing herself to this heavenly vengeance.

There was a great deal of truth in what the father said after a while: 'Were it not for your romance with his father we wouldn't have given him Fadia.'

It was an accusation which the mother continued to deny. She merely answered: 'Let him and his father go to Hell.'

This, however, did not alter the fact that she was once in love with the father of her daughter's husband, to whom they were related. This was found out by her husband one night when they were in bed together and she, in a moment of abandon, had called out the name of the relative instead of that of the person in whose embrace she lay.

Across Three Beds in the Afternoon

'Who do you think he looks like?' he asked for the hundredth time.

'I swear he doesn't resemble his father at all,' she answered, also for the hundredth time.

Then, remembering: 'Would you like me to make you a cup of coffee, Daddy?'

Without averting his eyes from the ceiling, Daddy asked:

'Hasn't Sayyid woken up yet?'

Sayyid was the only one who derived full benefit from the afternoon nap. He would sleep deeply for an hour or more, and on getting up would begin the evening's programme by drinking some coffee – an uninterrupted habit ever since he had taken his licentiate and joined the firm which had later become a governmental organization.

What would happen was that Sayyid would choose this moment to turn over on his bed and stretch out his legs to the full; he would then fling out his arms in a deep yawn, at which the father and the mother would intone with one voice:

'Had a good sleep, darling?'

Sayyid would mutter: 'Bless you', directed to the two of them.

'Did you sleep well?' the mother would ask.

'Not bad,' he would answer.

On this day, at the moment that Sayyid awoke from sleep, there immediately came to him the picture of the Head of the Department's room as he rose to his feet with flushed face to announce in a peremptory voice: 'An enquiry must be held.'

But it was the Head of the Department who was

The Smell of it

responsible for everything that had occurred. No sooner had he disdainfully announced that the question of dating letters was of extreme triviality and did not require all this discussion than Sayyid had jumped to his feet – perhaps for the first time in his career – to insist that many things depended on this trivial matter and that anyway it was an attempt to combat ignorance and indifference. This was an allusion which Soleiman regarded as an insult to himself, so he replied with a reference to Sayyid's chin on which no hair had until now appeared. And so Sayyid had raised his hand, certainly for the first time in his life, and slapped Soleiman on the face.

He was snatched away from the room of the Head of the Department by his father's voice saying: 'What do you say about Sayyid going off on his own and bringing the child back with him?'

He had for a long time past, owing to the affirmations of doctors, lost hope in having his name perpetuated on earth through Sayyid. Despite the fact that Fadia's child would not bear his name, he would, of course, carry a large part of his own blood – and here he was, at death's door, being deprived of seeing him.

When thinking about the new suggestion, the mother felt that complete victory over her daughter's husband would not be realized. He had a sort of assurance about their weakness and the best thing would be for them to find a way of forcing him to bring the child submissively – or at least to allow Fadia to do so.

'And will he accept?' she said without enthusiasm. 'In any case I'll tell Fadia if she rings.'

Across Three Beds in the Afternoon

They were all thinking about the same subject when the father said in an unconcerned tone:

'I wonder what will happen to the flat?'

The flat was a large one, consisting of the first floor of an old house with a garden, though its furnishings were all new.

'Perhaps they'll let it off furnished,' said the mother, 'or leave it for one of his brothers.'

'And when they return they'll find all the furniture ruined,' said the father anxiously.

They had known the furniture well, piece by piece, ever since the father and mother themselves had bought it – all except for the massive American refrigerator which their daughter's husband had brought from God knows where.

'Perhaps he'll only stay a year in Kuwait,' she said, 'and then there'll be no point in letting it off.'

'In that event,' said Sayyid, translating into words the thought that had appeared on the horizon, 'they can give us the refrigerator instead of leaving it in a closed-up flat.'

Over the past fifteen years the father had managed, from his meagre pension and Sayyid's salary, to provide his household, consecutively, with a Butogas, a waterheater, a hand shower, and a telephone – and finally a television, the instalments on which he was still paying off.

Every time they decided to buy a refrigerator he would stand beside the old wooden ice-box and, patting its surface, would say that it could carry on for the next summer and the best thing was to buy something else.

It was Sayyid who used to buy the ice for it twice a

The Smell of it

day in the summer, which they would place above its pipes; in the winter it was left unused for the cockroaches to sport about in.

'Fridges in Kuwait are dirt cheap,' said the father, 'and they could bring a new one back with them.'

'Everyone there owns a car,' said Sayyid.

The mother imagined Sayyid in a fast red car before the door of the house.

Sayyid was thinking about the clippers of the electric shaver which had gone wrong some time ago. It was one of the three gadgets he had bought from Gaza during one of the trips the organization used to arrange for its employees before June 1967. When the clippers had broken he had put the shaver away because there were no spare parts for it available on the market. (The other two gadgets he had also bought for twice their proper price.)

'Shall we have some coffee now?' said the mother with a sigh.

'By all means,' said the two of them together.

Sayyid left his bed and passed his fingers through his hair, then he went to the bathroom. When he returned to the room his mother had prepared the pot of coffee and had poured out three glasses; Sayyid distributed them round and each settled down anew on his bed.

'Perhaps they'll like it there and settle down in Kuwait,' the father continued the conversation.

Immediately the matter took on a new dimension in their minds. No one, however, dared to translate this dimension into words. Each one merely began to imagine summer afternoons in the garden, seated

Across Three Beds in the Afternoon

outside on rush chairs with a gentle breeze blowing whose coolness increased as the night advanced; or winter mornings on the other side of the house with the sun falling hesitatingly at first, then becoming increasingly warm as the day wore on.

It was the father who after a while said: 'Why don't we get in touch with Fadia and enquire how she and the child are? After all, he is our child.'

'I couldn't bear it if he answered,' replied his wife.

Her voice, though, was gentle when she added: 'If she hasn't rung within an hour I'll do so.'

Sayyid finished his cup of coffee and lit a cigarette. 'Aren't you thinking of going out, child?' his father asked him.

Sayyid did not usually go out in the afternoon, yet his father used to address this same question to him every day, and every day Sayyid would answer: 'No. I'll stay at home.'

For fifteen years this answer had filled the father's heart with sadness, for while other young men of his age would dress and spruce themselves up and run after girls, then marry and have children, Sayyid had suddenly begun, while still at school and university, to lose the great vitality which had distinguished him, and would lounge around the house silently drinking coffee and smoking while he read novels and looked at television.

With the passage of time the father had forgotten these old feelings and now, when he said to Sayyid, 'Go out son for a while instead of shutting yourself up here,' he had come to feel a sense of contentment and happiness when the other replied: 'And where shall I

103

The Smell of it

go? There's nothing I like better than sitting at home.'

Thereby both the father and the mother were assured that at the appropriate time they would obtain the necessary medical aid if they were to have one of the attacks that had begun to afflict them of late. It was truly strange that these attacks did not occur during the morning period when Sayyid was at the organization, but invariably came on after noon, and in particular at night after Sayyid had gone off to bed.

Then one of them would shout out 'Oh my!' and the next second Sayyid would be at the bedside asking what was wrong, dispensing medicine, and hurrying off to the telephone to get in touch with the doctor, who would make light of the matter in a bored voice and order a repeat of the same medicine on the prescription.

Sayyid's role did not end there. At the earliest opportunity, and on the instructions of the father and mother who generally took to their beds at one and the same time, he would start contacting the members of the family, one after another, to announce the news in that usual matter-of-fact voice: 'Actually, they're both a little unwell,' or 'They've both been in bed since yesterday.' In order to rebut the suspicion of having exaggerated he'd add: 'The doctor says ...,' then: 'What? Yesterday while we were asleep,' and would mention in detail what had happened.

Then the three of them would lounge about on their beds awaiting the reaction.

The father had turned over on to his left side and was facing the hall. 'See what's on the television tonight,' he said.

Sayyid searched around for the morning paper and

Across Three Beds in the Afternoon

found that it had fallen down behind his father's bed; he took it to his own bed, spread it out on the sheet, and began reading out aloud the evening's programmes.

The father was hoping that one of the old films the television had taken to showing of late would be on. How marvellous the young Abdul Wahhab was when he would button up his jacket, set his tarboosh on his head tipped slightly to the left, then, passing the palm of his hand across the hair along the right edge of the tarboosh, begin to sing; or Yusuf Wahbi when he gathered the ends of his robe around him, stood up to his full height, and roared out in his magnificent voice that a girl's honour was like a matchstick that could only be lit once!

Then, leaving his bed, he would seat himself directly in front of the television in order to be able to see properly, with Mummy on his right and Sayyid on his left, having put out the light, all three of them leaning on the table with their elbows until the evening's viewing was over.

Outside the darkness gathered quickly. Sayyid got up and put on the light and went back to poring over the newspaper.

'Fadia hasn't rung yet,' said the mother.

The father lay out straight on his back, his eyes once again coming to rest on the ceiling without distinguishing its features. 'We'll get in touch with her if she hasn't rung up in an hour's time,' he said.

Then:

'What are you giving us to eat this evening?'

Songs of Evening

أغاني المَسَاء

Songs of Evening

When the fat man appeared at the window I realized that the day had come to an end and that my father's voice would soon be calling me in. The fat man was carrying a long hose which came out from inside his flat. He took hold of it by the end and pointed it into the alleyway. We moved away from the circle of marbles and kept in close to the wall. I heard my friend cursing him in a low voice. The man composedly leant his arm on the window ledge and scanned the alleyway as though searching for the most suitable place from which to begin. Our eyes were glued on the muzzle of the hose, and when the water shot out of it we jumped in surprise, following the water as it flooded the area in which we had dug our five circles for the marbles; we saw the water flowing into the circles where the marbles were.

A moment later the alleyway, which a little while before had been filled with an ear-splitting noise, was completely empty. As the water poured out from the hose sweeping all before it, darkness fell and I looked upwards. The longer I directed my gaze upwards so the darkness lessened and I was able to see my father's

The Smell of it

face looking down at us from the balcony of our flat. I could make out his white skull-cap and the blueness of his eyes.

I heard his voice calling to me as he did every night and, as on every night, I felt a sadness. I gave the marbles to my friends, keeping a blue one, and walked to our house and climbed the long, narrow stairway.

I found the door of our flat open, with no one inside except for my father, who was still on the balcony. I made my way to the kitchen. I could hear my sister's voice coming from the next-door flat where she had gone to play with Umm Zakiyya's children. I washed myself at the kitchen tap, and hurried out to the balcony.

It was now pitch black outside and the light from the hallway was falling on the balcony. My father, however, was seated in the dark part of it. I stood at the balcony door for a moment and cast a glance at my father. I felt happy about him: the blueness of his eyes was limpid, and after a while I could make out the remainder of his features. His face was calm and relaxed, the expression dreamy and composed.

I seated myself silently alongside him. I was tired. He was deep in his reflections. From time to time his eyes came to rest on one of the lighted windows facing us, when he would follow what was to be seen through it as he puffed with relish at his cigarette.

I heard a movement behind me in the hallway: my sister had come from Umm Zakiyya's. My father hugged her to him and seated her on his lap. However, she announced she wanted to go to sleep. Putting her down on the floor, he stood up. He accompanied her

Songs of Evening

inside, and returned a little later. He took the pitcher of water we had placed on the edge of the balcony to get cool, removed its cover, and began swallowing the water with a gentle gurgling sound.

My ears picked up the sound of the radio in Umm Zakiyya's flat. I got up, saying: 'I'm going to bed. Sleep well, Dad.'

My father had seated himself in his chair. I came up to him, leant over, and kissed him on the cheek. 'And you, too,' he said.

I crossed the small hallway, which contained nothing but a wicker rocking-chair that had long ago come apart and a large wall clock. Entering our bedroom, I found my sister fast asleep, lying on her back with her long golden hair falling around her head, one leg bent upwards and the other across it. I stretched out my hand and put out the light, then I walked towards the bed, climbed into it, and stretched myself out alongside my sister. A slight breeze blew in on my face from the small window facing me, and I closed my eyes.

I used to like to go to sleep each night in the dark with the window open and the sound of the radio reaching me clearly from Umm Zakiyya's flat, the window of which adjoined ours. Umm Zakiyya only put on the radio when her children had gone to bed and she was sitting waiting for her husband. He was a quiet, shy man with a squint whose presence one was scarcely conscious of and who spent the whole day away from home. I once heard my father express surprise at what had brought him together with his plump, fair-skinned wife.

The sound of the radio came through clearly and I

The Smell of it

realized that their window was open. I listened with pleasure. Generally it would be Umm Kulthoum who would be singing. I did not know what she was saying. I was never able to make out the words of any song, in fact it would often happen that I would get muddled up between Abdul Wahhab, Mohammed Amin, and Farid al-Atrash, being interested only in the music itself.

I slowly opened my eyes and looked through the window. The sky was very close and the stars twinkled gaily, while one of them palpitated weakly, restively. Suddenly the radio went silent; I heard a movement in the next-door flat and realized that Abu Zakiyya had returned. After a short while his wife's voice could be heard, sometimes from close by, then from far away. The primus stove began giving out a low humming sound and then stopped. I heard the sound of a spoon striking a plate, and the woman's voice went on coming from the same place; it was a gentle voice that rang out clearly in the quietness of the night. I closed my eyes. This used to happen every evening. I continued listening to the humming sound that came from the next-door flat. I used to love that sound too, loved to go to sleep with it in my ears.

However, I did not fall asleep, for suddenly there rang out the long, intermittent sound of a siren. I opened my eyes wide. Realizing it was the air-raid warning, I began listening to it with enjoyment. My sister woke up in terror. I heard my father calling to me as he stumbled about in the darkness.

'I'm here, Dad,' I said to him. I grabbed my sister by the arm saying, 'Don't be frightened.'

Songs of Evening

Then we got down from the bed and made our way to the door, which showed up clearly; I made out my father's form in the darkness and went towards him. He spread out his arms to us and embraced us. He turned in the direction of the balcony and we moved towards it. Disorder reigned in the alleyway as the lights in the flats were hurriedly extinguished. Through the darkness I was able to make out the voices of the people hurrying down the stairs to the shelters. Raising my head to my father, I asked: 'Aren't we going to the shelter?'

I felt him smiling and I saw the blueness of his eyes in the darkness.

'What's the point of a shelter? Can anyone escape from what is ordained?'

My father shook his head as he burst out: 'Put your trust in God,' then raising his head skywards, pointed his finger peremptorily. I followed the movement of his finger with my eyes. There were thousands of stars close by – our flat was on the top floor and there was nothing above us but the roof.

All at once the siren stopped and an encompassing silence reigned over the whole world: I could hear the noise made by the air rustling my father's galabia.

My father drew us inside by the hand and we made our way cautiously to the bedroom, where we seated ourselves on the bed, and my father went over to the small window and closed it. Then, having thought a while, re-opened it, saying:

'Just in case the glass should fall out.'

'How can it fall out?' I asked him.

The Smell of it

'If a bomb was to fall nearby,' he said, 'the vibration would make it fall.'

'You never know,' I said; 'it might fall on us.'

'No, it won't,' he said confidently. 'Don't be frightened.'

I was not frightened. Approaching the window, I raised my hand slightly so as to rest it on the sill. My head was only slightly higher than the sill itself. I glanced at Umm Zakiyya's window and found it in darkness. I gazed up at the sky. Everything was quiet. I began to wonder about these raids in which nothing whatsoever happened. 'Look, Dad,' I called suddenly.

The searchlights had made their appearance in the sky. My sister hurried up alongside me, wanting to see. My father lifted her up, holding her under her arms so she could have a look. The searchlights were whirling feverishly through the sky, searching haphazardly. Suddenly two of them came to rest on a bright dot.

'They've caught a plane,' said my father from above us, but immediately added: 'Oh, the plane's got away.'

Again the searchlight moved quickly. Then, all of a sudden, they disappeared. I wondered where they'd gone to. Suddenly there rang out the faint, distant sound of an explosion. I felt my father's hand violently grip my shoulder; his galabia shook alongside my head and I realized that my sister was pulling him.

'Come along – it's better over here,' he said.

Dragging a blanket from off the bed, he got down on to his knees. He crawled under the bed and spread the blanket out on the stone floor, then called to us to join him. Quickly my sister and I crawled under the bed beside him. He was sitting with his head bent

Songs of Evening

forward so as not to bump it against the underneath of the bed. We packed in beside him and he hugged us in his arms. My sister and I were laughing. We could not see his face in the darkness but we heard him say:

'If a bomb were to fall on us now we'd fall on top of the people in the shelter. Nothing would happen to us but they'd be in a real mess.'

I was restive, being anxious to see what was going on in the sky. I crawled to the edge of the bed by the window. Putting my head out, I looked upwards and saw a part of the sky through the window. I continued gazing out expectantly. There were many stars and I fixed my eyes on each to make sure it was not moving. Soon I was quivering with joy: I had seen a large star that was gliding along and I realized it was an Israeli plane. I didn't want to utter a word in case my father stopped me watching. I went on looking at the aeroplane as it made its slow progress. Suddenly a number of searchlights made their appearance, converging and embracing, then drawing apart, rising and falling around the aeroplane as they surrounded it. It seemed to me that the aeroplane changed course. In order to see better, I closed my eyes for a moment, then opened them. Four searchlights were sweeping the sky around it, slowly and decisively drawing in on it from the four directions.

'Where have you got to?' whispered my father. 'Come here.'

I moved back beside him under the bed and we clung together, waiting in silence, The stillness was all-pervading, though we could hear a far-off rumbling sound that drew nearer moment by moment. It

The Smell of it

sounded as though it came from all four directions. For the first time I felt fear. Suddenly the rumbling stopped, after which we heard the sound of a nearby explosion. I clung to my father and he vigorously pulled me to him. My sister began crying. A series of loud explosions followed one another.

Suddenly my father crawled out, pulling us behind him, and we followed in silence. We moved in the darkness to the hallway, then towards the front door. It occurred to me that he was going to take us down to the shelter. However, he didn't open the door, but passed by it towards the lavatory, the door of which he opened. Small drops of water were dripping from the tap. My father gathered up the end of his galabia and, leaning forward, firmly closed the tap, then took out a box of matches and struck one, which lit up the lavatory. We saw where the round hole was and the two projecting bits on each side of it in the shape of feet; it also had a high stone base. My father raised the match above him and got on to the base. Then he turned round to us and, leaning his back against the wall, placed his feet on the two projecting feet alongside the lavatory hole, and pulled my sister up and stood her on his right-hand side. The match went out and he stretched his hand towards me and said: 'Up you come,' and I took hold of his hand and climbed up and stood on his left. Bending forwards, he drew the door towards us and shut us in.

We stood there in complete darkness, though I was aware of the difference between the dark brown colour which the walls of the lavatory were painted up to half-way and the whiteness of the upper parts; in fact,

Songs of Evening

I was aware of the brown colour shining in the darkness, the reason being, perhaps, that it had been done over with an oil paint. I was also conscious of the smell of the lavatory, which was predominantly that of whitewash and oil paint, since the flat was new and we had not lived in it more than a matter of months.

I could not hear anything at all. After a while I made out the sound of my father's heavy breathing; my head was resting against his side and I could feel his chest moving. My ear rubbed against a piece of metal in the truss he wore round his waist, and it hurt me. Soon we heard the sounds of a series of explosions; the sound was very near, as though in the adjoining street. I pictured to myself an aeroplane coming towards the house and letting drop its bombs. For the first time I found myself expecting that a bomb would fall on us at any moment.

My father's hand pulled me violently to his side and I clung closely to him. I was afraid. I was facing the draught from the door, so I turned and hid my face in his clothes. Touching his galabia, I kissed the cloth. I felt him shiver and heard him call out loudly: 'Gracious God!'

I do not know how long we stayed like this. Soon, however, I realized that the explosions had stopped. My father's grip on my shoulder relaxed and his breathing became less heavy. The quietness continued for some time, then the siren rang out shrilly, and my father rose to his feet and gave an audible sigh of relief. He lifted his hand from my shoulder and leaned over to the lavatory door and opened it, then he went down into the hallway and quickly put on the light. Meanwhile I

The Smell of it

hurried along behind him, with my sister calling out to me to wait for her till she had climbed down.

My father stood in the hallway under the light of the lamp. He took from his pocket one of his black cigarettes and began to light it. I was standing directly in front of him watching him; his eyes were now quite bloodshot.

My sister pulled me by the hand. She wanted to go to sleep and was frightened to go into the bedroom alone. My father silently made his way to the balcony, while I followed my sister into our bedroom. I put on the light and waited until she had climbed into bed, then I put it out and climbed in after her and stretched myself out in the darkness.

I tossed and turned. I listened anxiously, waiting to hear the radio that I might go to sleep to the sound of singing. The radio, however, was silent and I heard not a sound from the next-door flat. I lay straight out on my back and looked towards the window: the sky was vast and the stars excessively tiny as they throbbed weakly. Without getting up and going to the window to see, I knew that Umm Zakiyya's flat was in darkness.